There's an "S" on My Back

"S" IS FOR SCOLIOSIS

Mary Mahony

Redding Press
PO Box 366
Belmont, MA 02478

Susan A. Pasternack, Editor

Illustrations ©Jon Wilson, barefoot illustration

Cover and interior design ©Tamara Dever, TLC Graphics, Folsom, CA, and Erin Stark, Stark Design Works, Waukesha, WI

Printed by Bang Printing, Brainerd, MN

Portrait on page 199 ©Joe Demb Photography, 59 Louise Rd., Belmont, MA 02478

Fiction
RL: 5

Library of Congress Catalog Card Number: 99-096108
ISBN 0-9658879-1-X

Dedication

This book is dedicated to the orthotists, who in their own quiet way play an extremely important role in the lives of many scoliosis patients. Treating scoliosis is often accomplished through a triangle of care: doctor, patient, orthotist. It is this geometric shape that leads to a successful outcome. We thank you for sculpturing many a brace and for taking the pains to mold it into something that is often both corrective and user-friendly.

Maisey's story would not have been possible without the generosity of the following people, who shared their own expertise and experiences to help me create Maisey's story accurately and responsibly.

A SPECIAL THANKS TO

John E. Hall, M.D.
Robert B. Winter, M.D.
Tom Colburn, C.O.
Erin Mahony
and
Susan Pasternack

Contents

CHAPTER ONE

Diving In

"Hurry up, Maisey! I'll meet you in the car. Dr. Lebhar is squeezing us in, so we can't be late. He just wants to check your back. It's nothing major, just a quick check."

That's my mom. My name is Maisey MacGuire and I live in Mayberry, Massachusetts, with my parents and two older brothers, Conor and Mark. Dr. Lebhar has been my pediatrician since I was a baby. He has also taken care of my brothers. His office is in a big house near the center of Mayberry, a small town west of Boston. You may be more familiar with a town nearby, Concord, because of its role in the Revolutionary War.

Just about everybody in Mayberry knows who Dr. Lebhar is. He even comes to my school, Greens Farms, sometimes and talks to Ms. Bennett, the school nurse. I've seen him here, and I feel very special when he calls me by name. I never knew what he and the nurse talked about until now. I think they talk about backs. Let me tell you why.

Last week Ms. Bennett asked all the fifth-grade girls and boys to come down to her office. My teacher, Ms. Staples, said that she had to check our spines (part of your back) for this thing called "scoliosis," which means whether or not all the things in your back are straight. Fortunately, the girls and boys were examined separately. The girls wore sports tops (some people call them sports bras) and I'm not sure, but I think the boys just pulled their shirts up.

My class went last and we even missed part of recess. I was not happy about that at all. Ms. Bennett explained to us why this scoliosis screening was important. She said that this was a way of monitoring our growth so that if our spine showed any signs of curving, it could be taken care of early to avoid more serious kinds of treatment. She never really explained what the more serious treatments were, and no one felt the need to ask. I must admit, I did kind of wonder.

After the little talk, Ms. Bennett had each girl stand on a piece of masking tape stuck to the floor and asked each one to move into a diving position.

I kept thinking to myself, "I sure hope everyone knows how to swim!"

Then Ms. Bennett just seemed to stare at each back, looking ever so carefully. Eventually, it was my turn. She seemed to take a lot longer with me and I was getting pretty uncomfortable being in that position so long. Finally, she told me that I could stand up.

"Thank you, Maisey," she said. "You can put your shirt back on now."

I was hoping that it meant my back was perfect, but there was a very tiny part of me that worried that maybe something was wrong.

Just before it was time to go home Ms. Bennett called up to my classroom on the loudspeaker and asked Ms. Staples if she could send me down to the office for a minute to get something. That made me very nervous. When I got to the nurse's office, Ms. Bennett explained that she had a note for me to give my mom. "Nothing to worry about, Maisey. I've already called your mom and told her it's coming."

She had sealed the note so I couldn't see what was in it.

On the way back to my classroom I was so distracted that I missed a step, tripped, and almost bumped my mouth. I was relieved that no one had seen these antics. When I finally got upstairs, I went right to my locker and put the note in my backpack. In class, my friend Jean started giving me the third degree as to why I had to go to the nurse. I like Jean a lot, but sometimes she is very, very nosy. This was one of those times. I pretended I didn't hear her and started reading my *Scholastic News*. I could feel her staring at me, but I wasn't about to give her my attention. Saved by the bell. It was time to go home.

Jean followed me out to my locker with more questions about the nurse, and then Ms. Staples came over and reminded me to give my mother the note from Ms. Bennett.

"Must be really serious," I thought to myself, "if even my teacher knows about it."

By this time Jean had given up and was racing down the hall to be the first one on her bus. I gathered my things together and headed for my own bus.

I guess I got on, because suddenly I heard Mr. Barrett, our bus driver, yelling at me.

"Maisey, Maisey, pay attention girl. It's your stop. Now hurry along or I'm going to be late for the high school students."

I was so distracted by my day that I almost missed my stop. As I hurried down the steps, I noticed my mom was waiting for me.

"What's she doing here?" I thought.

She hadn't met me at the bus for almost two years. As we walked up the street toward my house, I waited for her to ask me for the note, but she didn't.

"That's weird," I thought.

. — .

When we got home I pulled out all my school papers and handed Mom the note from Mrs. Bennett.

"Oh, thank you, Maisey. I'll need this to give to Dr. Lebhar. The nurse wants him to check your back. Why don't you sit down and have a snack, and I'll explain to you what he's checking for."

As I sat there eating my cookies, Mom said that there is this thing called scoliosis. I told her that the nurse had used the same word when she checked our backs that morning in school. Mom got out the encyclopedia and showed me a picture of a spine that looked OK. Then she went to another page and showed me a picture of one that looked a little bit different, kind of cockeyed and bent. She explained that no one had to look like that anymore because there were doctors who could do special things to change the crooked-looking spines. It sounded almost like they had special powers. I was glad that she had shown me the pictures.

Even though Mom made it sound OK, like it was no big deal, I was still worried. I was getting bigger, and I hated it when I had to take off my shirt at the doctor's. It was kind of embarrassing. I was also hoping that Mom wouldn't tell my brothers. I didn't want them to be asking me about what Dr. Lebhar was going to do. Sometimes they can be a real pain. I was hoping that all three of us wouldn't have to traipse over to the doctor's together. Hopefully, Mom and I could do it when my brothers were at sports.

Later, when Dad arrived home from work, he came right up to my room. Usually, he just calls up to me when he gets home and then hangs around the kitchen talking to Mom while she puts the finishing touches on our dinner. We tend to eat late because our dad has kind of an important job that doesn't let him out too early. Dad is a mechanical engineer, and he always says that if he didn't stay late at the office, his boss wouldn't think that he was so important. I don't quite follow his thinking on that, but I guess it's one of those parent things.

Dad was very different that night. I knew he wanted to say something to me. I was pretty sure it was about my back. He didn't seem to know how to begin and I didn't feel much like giving him a jump start. He kept repeating himself and eventually gave up, and we headed down to dinner.

Dinner was not very exciting. My brothers always find something to disagree about — salt, pepper, bread, dessert. You name it, they argue about it. My older brother, Conor, is a freshman in high school and seems to know everything about anything. My other brother, Middle Mark, is in seventh grade and likes people to think that he smiles a lot. He really isn't a "steady smiler," I used to want to tell people, but why waste my breath.

This night was no different. Conor wanted the last roll, but Mark said it was his turn to have it. Dad settled the argument by eating it himself. I got to have dessert first. That was kind of weird, too, my getting dessert first.

When I went to bed, Mom and Dad both came in to kiss me good night. Mom reminded me that she had made an appointment with Dr. Lebhar for the next day and that it would only take a few minutes. We would go right after school. Dad's only comment was, "Don't worry, Maisey."

Somehow I had the feeling that he was already worrying. Then they each gave me a big hug and kiss and said good night.

I lay in the dark for a long time thinking about my back. It didn't hurt. When I looked in the mirror it seemed to look OK.

"What's the big deal?" I thought to myself.

In a way it was kind of annoying. I had just gotten braces put on my teeth and now I had to go to yet another doctor. I was hoping that I wouldn't have to keep seeing Dr. Lebhar as much as Mom made me see the dentist.

"Sometimes being a kid can be really tough," I thought.

The next morning I overslept a bit and so everything was rush, rush, rush. In a way I was kind of glad. Mom reminded me that I had to hurry after school and eat a quick snack, so that I wouldn't be late for the doctor. I kind of wished that she hadn't said anything in front of my brothers.

"Why is Maisey going to the doctor?" they both chimed in.

"He just wants to check her back. Nothing serious," Mom replied.

I grabbed my backpack and darted out the door to the bus. I sure didn't want to hang around for what they might have in store for me.

My school day went pretty quickly. We had lots of specials like art, gym, and a program on Native Americans, so it was an easy day. The bus ride home went fine and before I knew it, I was walking in the door of my house to the smell of homemade brownies. Mom knew just what I liked. I had my snack and ran upstairs to brush my teeth. I kind of took my time brushing. Somehow, I wasn't in the same big hurry that my mom was.

"Maisey, Maisey, come on," yelled my mom. "We are going to be so-o-o late! The boys are being dropped off from soccer practice in an hour so we have to go right now."

As I got into the car, I was not at all excited about this visit. I had mentioned it in school to Jean, and she said she knew someone who had one of those crooked spines and the girl had to wear a big, clumsy brace. She couldn't even wear her designer jeans. After Jean said that I had wondered why I ever told her what was wrong. Sometimes she can be "Mean Jean."

It was a short ride to Dr. Lebhar's office. He is located right behind the post office, so there is usually a parking space. You really aren't supposed to use the post office spaces, but Mayberry is a small town and no one makes a big deal of it.

Since Dr. Lebhar was squeezing us in, I was hoping it wouldn't be a long wait. His office was pretty full, and most of the kids had gooey or crunchy noses and bad coughs. It was late fall, and the germs seemed to have running shoes. Up until today, I never thought of myself as a sickly kid. I wasn't sure if the spine got sick, but I was certain Dr. Lebhar would know.

"Your turn, Maisey. Come right in," said Mrs. Johnson.

Ms. Johnson had been Dr. Lebhar's nurse for as long as I could remember. She had a special way about her and often talked to me about school as I got undressed. I think she knew I got embarrassed and so she always gave me a gown to put on. This particular day she called my mom in before I even got undressed. I was kind of annoyed about that, but I knew they had made special time for us.

"Just take your shirt off, Maisey, and leave your pants on," said Ms. Johnson. "You can put the gown on over your pants with the opening at the back. Dr. Lebhar only needs to see your back today."

While I stood behind the screen undressing, I could hear Mom and Ms. Johnson talking about scoliosis. Ms. Johnson told my mom that it was very common at my age to see this happening.

"Common," I thought to myself. "I don't know a lot of kids with it, and I know a lot of kids!"

Just then the door opened and Dr. Lebhar came in. As he greeted my mom, he called to me, "Come out here, Maisey, and let's see what's up with your back."

Even though we were only in there for ten minutes, it seemed like hours. He asked me to bend over and repeated what the nurse had done the day before in school. He asked my mom to come close and showed her the area they were talking about. Dr. Lebhar confirmed that Ms. Bennett was right and that there was a slight "S" curve to my spine.

"S," I thought to myself. "Now my back has a letter on it!"

"Maisey, this is nothing to worry about. You are beginning your preadolescent growth spurt, which is often when this happens. I'm going to send you on to see another doctor, an orthopedist. He specializes in scoliosis, and he will decide what needs to be done. He's going to take some pictures of your spine called X rays, and then he'll sit and talk to you about them. He's a wonderful doctor, and I'm sure you're going to like him," said Dr. Lebhar.

While I put my shirt back on, Mom went out with Ms. Johnson and Dr. Lebhar to set up the appointment with the back doctor. I could hear them talking outside the door, and I thought I heard the word "brace," but I couldn't be sure. It was all kind of scary.

. — .

The ride home was very quiet and even though Mom kept trying to get me to talk, I didn't feel like it. She told me that in two weeks we'd be going to see the orthopedist. He works in a big hospital in Boston. We only go into Boston for special events like plays and ice shows. Even though seeing this new doctor would be a special event, it really didn't belong in the same category.

Once we got home, my brothers had a million questions. I really hated that. I knew they meant well, but they always exaggerated things. Finally, Mom sensed my discomfort and told them to go out and play until dinner. I went up to my room and read my library book.

Dinner is usually the time for family talk in our house. When Dad got home, he came right up to my room again to say hello and asked me how the appointment went. Before I got a chance to answer, Mom called us for dinner.

"Oh darn," I thought, "now this will be dinner talk."

Fortunately, Mom didn't go into a lot of detail, which I knew meant that she and Dad would talk later. Dad tried to make me feel better and told me that he had a friend whose daughter also had scoliosis. He explained how she wore a brace for a few years and then her back improved. I know he was trying to be kind, but I could see my brothers' eyes start to twinkle at the word "brace."

"Here we go," I thought.

CHAPTER TWO

A Second Opinion

The next few weeks were uneventful. Jean pretty much stopped bugging me in school about my back. My brothers were finishing up their soccer season — Conor on the freshman team at our regional high school and Mark on the town team. All they could think about was soccer, soccer, soccer. A few times I heard my mom talking to her two best friends on the phone about my back, but I couldn't hear exactly what she was saying. In a way, I was glad I couldn't. Mom has lots of friends, and I guess it's OK for her to share with them since I share with my friends, too; well, most of the time.

Finally, the day arrived for our visit to the orthopedist. I could hardly say the word. I was allowed to take the day off from school since it was a morning appointment. I knew my mom had told Ms. Staples about it because she had given me homework for two nights the day before. Then she proceeded to tell me that if I didn't get it done it would be all right.

"Thanks a lot," I thought to myself. "If I don't need to do it, then why are you giving it to me?"

The drive into Boston was long, over an hour. The highway we took, Route 2, is always backed up in the morning, and, when we finally got out of that, the traffic in Boston was very heavy, and Mom wasn't as good as Dad at maneuvering in it. Finally, she opened her window and started motioning to people for permission to cut in. At one point she even told a driver that her daughter had a doctor's appointment. How embarrassing. When he peered inside the car to see if I looked sick, I wanted to crawl under the seat. I was relieved when we finally reached the hospital parking garage.

Finding the doctor's office was like going through a maze. So many signs, people rushing about, and a very unusual smell to the whole building. That same smell that was in Dr. Lebhar's office. The doctor's waiting area was huge. I had just gotten comfortable when the secretary came over and told us that I had to go to the X-ray department.

The X-ray waiting area was packed. There were all sorts of kids there, some in braces, some in wheelchairs, and lots of very serious moms and dads. My mom, who was usually very friendly, became unusually quiet.

"This is so unlike her," I thought.

Finally, it was my turn. A nurse came out and walked me to a room where I was asked to take off my clothes and put on a gown. We then went into another room that had a big table. Inside the large room was a smaller one, kind of like a booth, with computers in one tiny part of it. Instead of asking me to get on the table, the nurse told me to stand up against the wall in a lot of different positions. I remember how cold her hands were when she touched my back. She was very friendly and said that she had had scoliosis herself as a child. She looked pretty good to me, so that made me feel a little bit better.

I wasn't allowed to get dressed until they finished developing the X rays. Soon the nurse told me I could go and handed my mom this huge, flat, rectangular package to bring to the doctor.

By the time we got back to the doctor's office, the waiting room had thinned out. The secretary took the X rays from Mom right away. Within ten minutes we were in Examining Room 2. I couldn't believe that once again I had to undress.

"It would have been a lot easier to have the X ray in the same place so that I only had to undress once," I thought.

When the doctor came in, Mom was friendly but quiet, and she looked like she was studying him. I was distracted by his very long name. He seemed to know this and with a laugh told me that I could call him Dr. Bones because that's the kind of doctor he is. I started to giggle and soon felt very comfortable with him. I liked having a funny doctor.

Dr. Bones spent a lot of time checking not only my back but the length of my legs, feet, and arms. He seemed to check just about everything that was attached to my back. He asked me a lot of questions about the things I like to do, whether or not I like school, and then he started asking me questions about my back. He even asked me if it ever hurt. Then he put my X rays up on a box with lights and showed my mom and me what my back was doing. He called it "idiopathic scoliosis" and said I had a primary curve to my spine that measured about 28°. Then he started talking about the same "S" that Dr. Lebhar had mentioned, but I could hardly see the "S" in the picture, and I still wasn't quite sure what a primary curve was. I knew that they called the early grades in school "primary grades," and I wondered if I had an "early back." If that was true, then what would a "later back" look like?

Dr. Bones must have been reading my mind because he began explaining that a primary curve is the bigger kind and that when I bent over he could tell that my spine was not as flexible as it should be.

Then he went on to explain that there is another kind of idiopathic curvature that is called "compensatory." That kind of curve is smaller and not as easy to see. It was all so confusing.

"Where does it come from?" asked my mom.

According to Dr. Bones, "idiopathic" means origin unknown. But in some cases, he said, "research has shown that it might be in the family somewhere. In other cases, it just appears."

Now I was even more confused. I guess Mom understood it all, because she told the doctor that no one in her family or my dad's family had ever had this problem. At least, no one that she knew of. Dr. Bones didn't seem to be at all surprised with that and just kind of smiled.

After Dr. Bones showed us the X rays, he sat me down.

"Maisey," he said, "This is what we need to do, but we need a lot of help from you. Since your curve is over 25°, we will need to put a brace on your back to see if we can stop it from curving any further. You will need to wear your brace most of the day. You can take it off for a few hours each day, but that's all. You can still play sports and do whatever else you normally do. This is very important. Hopefully, the brace will stop your spine from any further curving."

And then he said, "Now Maisey, if you have any questions, this is a good time to ask them."

I had a lot of questions, but there were two big ones that I *really* wanted an answer to. "How long will I have to wear the brace and what happens if the brace doesn't work?"

Dr. Bones just kind of smiled again.

"Well, Maisey, would you believe me if I told you that almost everyone asks those questions? I can't really tell you in months or years about the brace, but I can suggest that by the time you stop growing, the brace will be gone. If, by chance, the brace does not work, we have other alternatives. But for now, let's just go with the brace and not worry about any of that."

He seemed pretty matter-of-fact about the whole thing, and Mom seemed relieved. I didn't feel one bit relieved. I had a feeling that no matter how I felt, this was something I was just going to have to do. It seemed so unfair.

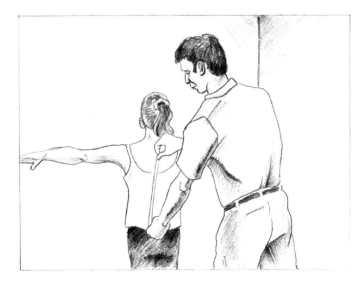

CHAPTER THREE

Brace Yourself

Dr. Bones made a quick call and asked us to go to another area to see someone called the "orthotist," who would make my brace. As we were moving out of the examining room, he quickly explained that an orthotist is a person with very special training who makes appliances for the body.

"Appliances," I thought to myself. "I hope they aren't going to plug me in." Dr. Bones then added, "You know, Maisey, medical appliances are things like braces."

I wasn't quite sure how this would happen but I had a feeling I was going to find out real soon. Mom gathered up my clothes, thanked Dr. Bones, and off we went.

When we got to the door, I noticed a big black plate on it that said "Casting Room." I could feel my stomach getting a little squeamish as I recalled the gory details of many of my friends' experiences with broken arms, wrists, and legs. As soon as the door opened my somewhat scary thoughts were distracted by a display of the assortment of colors you could choose for your cast. Immediately, I set my sights on neon pink. In the background, I heard my mom introducing herself to someone, and I looked over and saw this young guy with a big smile on his face.

"What is he so happy about?" I thought to myself.

"Hi, Maisey. My name is Tom, and I'm going to be making your brace today. I can see that you have noticed all the colors available for casts. Unfortunately, our back braces only come in white and very white," he said, half chuckling.

Somehow I didn't think it was that funny. I was pretty disappointed. Sensing that I was not very happy to be there, Tom explained to me what he was going to do.

"Maisey, I'm just going to take some measurements of your body," he said.

As Tom worked he explained to Mom and me that he had had scoliosis, too, and that when he was about my age he had also been put in a brace. That really got my mom started with her twenty questions, and I was kind of annoyed that he started talking more to her than to me.

He asked me to stand as steady as possible while he measured my body. I could tell by one look on my mom's face that she was even more blown away than I was by all this. She kept asking Tom the same question but rewording it each time in a different way. What she really wanted to know was whether I really had to be braced.

Tom was very quick, and within no time he was done. Then he took Mom and me into another room, letting us see what the brace was going to look like after he finished making it. I was feeling angry and very uneasy. The braces looked really scary, and the whole thing was beginning to sink in. None of the other kids in my class had to wear anything like this. It was going to be so embarrassing.

"Don't worry, Maisey," said Tom. "It's not going to be that bad at all. You'll learn all the things you need to do to make it as comfortable as possible. Besides, baggy clothes are in style."

"Is he crazy?" I thought. "I never wear baggy clothes. And what does he mean 'don't worry!'"

While I went into the bathroom, Mom stayed with Tom. When I came out, she announced that we would be going shopping soon for some new clothes. That was a clue that she was really upset, because Mom never just took us shopping, except at the beginning of the school year. Besides, she usually sewed my skirts and jumpers. I was feeling tired and just wanted to go home. We said good-bye to Tom and were on our way.

When we got to the car, I could tell that Mom wanted to talk, but I really didn't feel like it. I knew Jean was going to want to know everything about my brace, and I was so dreading having to wear it to school. I was not at all in a hurry to get it. Gym is one of my favorite activities in school, and I knew this was going to make it really yucky.

Mom was having a hard time, herself, because all of a sudden she said, "Maisey, I know this is hard for you, and I want you to know that it's hard for me, too. Surprises are not always easy. But before you begin to worry, let's just wait until the brace comes. It might not be that bad at all."

I felt like she was inside my head.

"How did she know I was worrying?"

Then I decided to close my eyes and pretend to be asleep. The next thing I heard was "Maisey, Maisey, wake up."

Mom was nudging me and telling me it was time to go inside. We were home.

CHAPTER FOUR

Sharing the News

Just as I was beginning to enjoy my peace in the house, my brothers came screaming in the back door.

"Maisey, what did you get at the hospital? Are you sick or something? Did you have to get a shot?"

Oh, they can be such a pain. Mom must have sensed that I did not want to be with them. She sent me upstairs to do my reading for school. I knew she was going to talk to them about my back.

"Thank you, Mom," I thought. "You can do the honors."

Trying to read was really hard. I just couldn't seem to concentrate. I felt like I was the only one in the world with an "S" on her back, even though I knew this wasn't true. I wanted to call one of my friends, but then again, maybe I would wait a while.

All of a sudden I felt the presence of someone in my room. I looked up to see my best friend, Molly, who had come over to say hi and to see if I wanted to have a neighborhood kickball game.

Molly is the best. She lives next door and is the youngest of three girls. Molly is also a fifth grader but she goes to a charter school in our town. She said her parents thought it would be a good experience for her. Molly says that charter schools are more flexible than regular schools and look at your creative side more. She calls it "experimenting with learning." I didn't really understand what they meant, but I remember that my mom said that they had the same stuff in Molly's school as mine but are allowed to use it any way they want.

What does it matter? Even though Molly doesn't go to

my school, we are still great friends. I often confide my deepest, darkest secrets to Molly, and she shares hers with me. Her parents are a lot older than mine, and they go away a lot. Molly spends lots of time with her grandmother, who is her babysitter. Her grandmother seems really, really old. I love going over to Molly's house, because her grandmother lets us do almost anything we want.

One Easter she let us buy a real, live duck and a little plastic pool for it to swim in. Molly told me later that her grandmother got in big trouble for that one, but it sure was fun. The duck simply disappeared one day, and Molly said her mother told her it was called to the pond where all ducks go. My brothers said that the pond was in the ground, but I didn't believe them.

"Maisey, where have you been all day?" Molly asked. "I called you earlier to see if you and your brothers wanted to play kickball, but no one answered."

"I had to go with my mom to see this special back doctor, because the school nurse and Dr. Lebhar say my back isn't straight."

Molly also goes to Dr. Lebhar, as do almost all the kids in our small town.

"Well, what do you call it?" Molly asked.

"It's a really big name that begins with an "S" and ends with an "S," I replied.

"But what is the whole name?"

Just as she finished her sentence my mom came into my room.

"It's called scoliosis, Molly," my mom answered.

"Mrs. MacGuire, my two big sisters had that," Molly said. "They had to wear braces and these really neat baggy clothes. They even got to wear sweatshirts to school whenever they wanted. Darcey had an operation and got all kinds of treats and could watch TV whenever she wanted for several weeks. She didn't even have to wash her hair. Meg didn't need an operation and just had to wear a brace for a few years. Even though she hated the brace, it worked."

I never thought much about Molly's sisters because they are a lot older than Molly and live far away. Both are married and Darcey is always in school because she's going to be a doctor. Molly's mother always says that Molly is her special gift and so I have never asked much about her sisters.

My mom jumped right in and asked Molly if her sisters would be coming home soon so that I could talk to them. Isn't that just like a mom.

"Maybe I don't want to talk to them," I thought.

I wanted to tell my mom to MHOB (mind her own business), but I didn't.

I just sat there kind of quiet. Mom seemed to get the message and finally left. I really wanted to be alone with Molly to ask her more questions, but I didn't want my mom to know.

Molly and I lay on my bed for what seemed like hours. She and I like many of the same things. When we first met that wasn't quite true. Molly was a wonderful reader, but I was what my reading teacher called "a developing reader," which was a different way of saying that I had a learning disability.

In those days, we played with dolls a lot and made up plays. Then my reading got better, and Molly started bringing books over and reading with me. She made a big sign that said "Molly Miller and Maisey MacGuire present Reader's Theatre." My mom and dad said that part of the reason I got better in reading was because of my reading teacher; the other part was Molly. I think they were right. Molly got me really excited about reading. She made it an adventure.

We never did get out and play kickball even though my brothers called up every five minutes to see if we would. I didn't feel much like playing anything. Mom even let Molly stay for dinner.

"Having a back problem may not be so bad after all," I thought. "But right now it seems pretty awful."

I could tell Molly read my mind, because she scrunched up her nose the way she always did when we were thinking the same thing.

The next day Mom drove me to school and, unfortunately, as I was getting out of the car, "Jean, Jean, the Gossip Queen" was getting out of the bus. She followed us in and saw that my mom was heading for the nurse's office.

"Oh darn," I thought. "Jean will be pumping me all day."

Part of me wanted to tell her about my back and just get it over with while another part of me wanted to keep it a secret forever. Amazingly, Jean didn't ask one question and the day was pretty normal.

At lunch everyone was talking about school pictures and what they were going to wear. I was relieved that the photographer was coming the next day. I didn't want my school pictures to include my new "appliance."

CHAPTER FIVE

Brace Day

Each day seemed to pass as normally as it did before scoliosis. I often heard my mom and dad talking quietly after dinner, but I couldn't hear exactly what they were saying. They did that before. It's kind of a mom-and-dad thing.

Finally, we couldn't put it off any longer. One weekend, my mom and I spent the whole Saturday shopping for new clothes that would fit over the brace. It took so long for me to find something I liked, but I knew I had to hang in there so that I would have clothes to wear. Mom was a real trouper. Most of the time I didn't like what she liked, but she didn't seem to mind. I knew she really hated shopping. On this particular day, so did I.

Eventually, we found some mix-and-match outfits that didn't thrill me, but I knew they would have to do. The doctor had said that it would not be the best time in my life when it came to my wardrobe. My mom said that was a big "understatement."

When we got home, I called Molly over and modeled my new wardrobe for her. She seemed a lot more excited about it than me. But Molly is such a great friend, and by the time she left, I was almost excited myself.

. — .

Brace day finally arrived, another one off from school. Missing school really bothers me because of my learning disability. When I first learned how to read, I would always reverse the letters in words, so the word "was" looked like "saw" to me. I just couldn't seem to get the letters in the right order or when I finally did, I couldn't remember how they sounded. They gave me a lot of help in school. Molly helped, too, bringing over books and making reading a fun time.

Although I am now a good student and my reading has really improved, I hate all the makeup work when I am absent. It takes me so long to get it all done. Also, it is hard to catch up on things with my friends. They never remember to tell you everything that happens when you're absent. You want the whole meal and you only get a taste. I suppose I do the same to them when they are out.

I knew getting my brace was a major event because my dad was coming along. It always makes me feel really important when both my parents come to something. I also knew my dad would spend most of the time reading his paper. My brothers and I are used to that.

When we arrived at the hospital we went through the same process as the first time. Park in garage. Cross street. Enter hospital. Go to second floor for registration, and then, the worst of all, wait *forever* for the doctor to see you.

The wait was long, as usual. I almost fell asleep. Dad kept getting up and pacing with this very serious look on his face. That meant he was getting impatient, which made Mom look more and more uneasy. No matter where we go, if we have a long wait, Dad always does the same thing, and Mom always gets that look.

Finally, the nurse came out and called my name. Dad went flying over, signaling to my mom and me to follow. I felt as if everyone was watching us.

"Cool your jets, Dad," I thought to myself.

I'm sure the nurse was thinking, "another pushy parent!"

As she escorted us to an examining room, Dr. Bones was right on our heels and greeted us as he closed the door. He introduced himself to my dad, said hello to my mom, and then came over to me with this big, warm smile on his face. Even though I was pretty upset about getting a brace, he made me feel good. He spoke to me as if I were the only person in the room.

Soon there was a tap on the door, and Tom the orthotist arrived with my brace. Dr. Bones was just putting up my X rays, showing my dad where the curve was in my spine. Tom came right over and presented my new piece of armor. All I needed was a helmet and a sword and I'd have the whole outfit! I was dreading this more than I can ever put into words.

I had mixed feelings. I was a little curious and part of me really wanted to try it on, but I was afraid once I got it on I wouldn't like it, and it would make me sad. Dr. Bones didn't waste any time and asked everyone to leave the room while I slipped on a special undershirt that Tom had brought. It felt both thick and soft. I stood there for a moment just looking at the shirt and the brace, thinking that this was far from the bra I had hoped to be wearing.

Suddenly Dr. Bones called in, "All set, Maisey?"

I quickly slipped into the undershirt, which I was pleased to see was long enough to cover my panties. Dr. Bones came in and carefully slipped the brace over my chest and then tightened it by pulling the Velcro straps in the back. Mom asked whether I could bend or sit down in the brace.

"Whoa, Mom," I thought to myself.

Dr. Bones smiled and asked me to step up to the examining table and try to sit down. When I did, the bottom of the cast cut across the tops of my legs. Tom quickly came to my rescue with a marking pen and announced that the brace needed a bit more trimming. Dr. Bones said that he would see another patient while we waited in the examining room for Tom to return. I was getting very, very tired of all the waiting. Fortunately, my dad offered to take a walk to find some snack food.

Before long Tom returned and behind him was Dr. Bones — the B & T Team. Tom carefully placed the brace over my body. It fit much better and I was feeling a tiny bit more positive about it. Well, not too much. There were a few no-no's: no contact sports, no trampoline, no skateboarding, no rollerblading. But I was allowed to take my brace off for three to four hours a day. At least I had that. It seemed I could pretty much do everything I had done before. At least that's what Dr. Bones said.

Dr. Bones sent me off to X ray with the brace on.

"Give me a break," I thought.

After a long wait, it was my turn. The technician explained how important it is to get an X ray in the brace so that Dr. Bones could see if the brace was doing its job.

I carried the X rays back to Dr. Bones's nurse and went into the examining room for one last check. Dr. Bones showed us the X ray and pointed out how much straighter the brace was holding me. Unfortunately, Dad missed the show because he was off getting my food.

When Dr. Bones left, Dad arrived with my snack, which I think he must have driven all the way home to get. Tom stayed around and explained brace care to us — rubbing alcohol on the skin to toughen it up, undershirt under the brace at all times, bath or shower daily when out of the brace, and last, but not least, air the brace out when not in use. I hadn't really thought much about whether or not it would smell until Tom mentioned it. Oh yuck!

While Dad went out to get the parking ticket stamped, Mom helped me get dressed. The elastic on the top of my underpants just fit over the brace.

"Maisey, this is the one thing we didn't think of," said Mom. "I'll pick up some larger underpants for you tomorrow."

My sweatpants with the elastic waist fit perfectly over the brace. I was glad that I had gotten a really baggy sweatshirt.

I glanced in the mirror in the hall as I left. I really didn't look that bad. You couldn't tell. Well, maybe just a little.

"Oh how I hate being in this thing," I thought to myself.

On the way home, Mom and Dad insisted that we go out to lunch. How I dreaded eating in the new cage, but I could tell they really wanted to go. Mom never turned down a lunch with Dad. The only other time they went out to lunch was on her birthday.

I was not very hungry. Dad managed to eat his food, taste Mom's, and finish mine. A regular disposal! You never left the table at home during dinner for fear that Dad would think you were done and eat the rest of your food. Once, one of my brothers had a friend over, my dad ate the rest of his meal while the friend left to go to the bathroom. When he returned, Dad had finished the boy's steak. The boy sat down and asked where it was.

Dad very quietly announced, "I ate it."

Mom didn't let Dad forget that for a long, long time.

When we got home, I told Mom that I wanted to go upstairs and read for a while. I locked my door, put all my clothes on the bed, and tried on every outfit in my closet to see how they looked. I should say I tried to try on the outfits. I couldn't fasten the button on any of my old pants. Forget the blouses and the skirts. Thank goodness the new outfits were OK. I really wanted Molly's opinion. Unfortunately, she was still in school. I really needed her.

The boys came up to my room as soon as they got home. I was really glad, because I wanted to hear what they had to say. Mom came up and took the brace off so that I could show them. Conor wanted to know if I could still have dessert or if it would make me bulge out in the brace. Mark wondered if he was going to need a brace some day. Considering that they could have really teased me, they were pretty nice. Today I really liked having brothers.

Molly came over just as we were sitting down to dinner. Mom invited her to join us. I couldn't believe it! That's twice in one month.

But Molly took one look at the beef stew and said, "No thanks, Mrs. MacGuire. I'll pass."

Conor whispered "dog food" and Mom threatened him with no dessert. I was disappointed that Molly and I couldn't be alone, but she did get to see me in the brace even though it was for just a minute.

After dinner I took my shower. It felt so good. My skin looked a tiny bit red under my arms and it did feel a little uncomfortable because I wasn't used to having something between my tummy and my clothes. I couldn't remember what Tom had said about this. I mentioned it to Mom when I got out of the shower and she suggested that these were pressure marks and that we dab them with rubbing alcohol. I was a little worried it would sting, but it actually felt good.

Soon it was time to get back into the brace, and I felt a bit like I feel when my vacation ends. It was just a harmless piece of plastic, but it felt so big on my small body. Mom was very careful and patient about putting it on so that it rested perfectly in place over my hips. At first she did the straps a bit too tight, but they were easy to readjust. Dad came in for a demonstration so that he could learn how to do it too. I could hear my brother Mark breathing through my door like Darth Vader, but I was not about to give him a show. I had to draw the line somewhere!

After Dad kissed me good night he went downstairs, which gave me a few minutes with Mom. I just needed a little reassurance that the brace was not that noticeable. I was feeling pretty teary about the whole thing, and I kind of wanted to cry. Mom seemed to know how I was feeling and gave me a big hug, telling me how proud she was of me and how hard she knew this was, not only for me, but for all of us. Suddenly, I could feel the tears tiptoeing down my cheeks. It felt so good to let go at last.

"Maisey, Maisey, let it out. You'll feel better," Mom whispered.

After a few minutes I did feel better and told Mom that I really wanted to try to go to sleep. What I wanted was to have a heart-to-heart with myself. I tried to think of what Molly would say. She always seemed to know.

CHAPTER SIX

Re-entry

The next morning Mom drove me to school, which really helped. She said she wanted us to stop in at the nurse's office to tell Ms. Bennett that I had the brace and also to show her how to help me when it hurt. Ms. Bennett would be the one taking it off for gym or whenever I needed a break. Dr. Bones had said I could divide up my four hours out of the brace any way I wanted, which made me feel pretty happy.

Ms. Bennett was very nice. We worked out a schedule for the first few weeks so that I could have at least one break from my brace each morning. I was a little nervous about going into class because I felt that everyone could tell I was a lot bigger looking. Ms. Bennett said that everyone feels odd when something is new. She asked me if I would mind if she came into my classroom some time to do a talk on braces of all kinds. She thought it would tie into our dental unit and also help me out. She promised that I did not have to speak or show my brace. I said I'd think about it. I was kind of in a hurry to get up to my classroom, and the last thing I wanted to think about was a brace presentation.

I felt a little like a stiff going up the stairs. Ms. Staples greeted me at the door to my classroom and Jean practically jumped over her desk to welcome me. "Very suspicious," I thought.

She followed me over to my desk and was extra nice. Finally, she looked me right in the eye and asked if it hurt. I suddenly remembered having told her that I was going to be out again on account of my back. I had mentioned that I needed to get a brace, but to keep it a big secret. I think I knew that she would never be able to keep it a secret and maybe I even wanted her to tell the others so that I wouldn't have to.

"No, it doesn't hurt," I answered. "Stop talking about it or everyone will start looking."

"Will you show me what it looks like later on?"

Jean is always so curious and in a way I really did want to show it to someone to see what they thought. I agreed to show it to her in the girls' room after recess.

. — .

The morning was just like any other at school. Recess was a little awkward. Hanging from the monkey bars with a brace on just wasn't the same. Ms. Staples looked over and quietly shook her head. I could feel the no-no's coming and this was only the first day. Jean hung out with me after that and kept asking me if I thought recess was almost over. I knew she wanted to go into the girls' room to see what my brace looked like.

We had to wait a few minutes for everyone to finish. Then, when the girls' room was almost empty, we went into the last stall and I lifted my shirt and showed her my new piece of armor.

"Maisey, that's really neat. Wow, I couldn't even tell how big it was because of your sweatshirt."

Jean really made me feel good.

On my way out Ms. Staples took me aside and suggested that I go down and get my brace off for gym. I couldn't wait. It felt like it was rubbing a tiny bit across the bottom of my stomach. Ms. Bennett was waiting and took me into the back bathroom for privacy. She was very gentle and after she took the brace off, I lifted the bottom of my undershirt to show her where it hurt. There was a big red mark and it was very sensitive. Instead of rubbing alcohol, she applied cornstarch and said we'd have to watch it carefully. We decided not to put the brace back on until after lunch, which came right after gym. I was so relieved. My skin felt so much better without the brace.

Lunch was pretty normal, and reluctantly I did share about my brace with the rest of the table. They had heard Jean asking me a question and after that the news was out. I'm pretty sure it was out long before that.

When I returned to Ms. Bennett after lunch, she handed me a note for my mother. She said that she was a little concerned about the mark on my tummy and she wanted my mother to watch it carefully. She explained that it takes the skin time to get used to the brace.

Soon I was on the bus riding home. Mom met me at the bus stop and drove me home. I was glad that she had brought the car. After a quick snack I vegged out on the rug in front of the TV, and the next thing I remember is Mom calling me to dinner.

CHAPTER SEVEN

A Routine

Just as we were about to eat dinner, Molly called. I was so excited to talk to her and tell her about my first day in the brace. I just needed to unload. Mom said that she could come over after dinner since we were having takeout pizza, and she hadn't ordered enough for anyone extra. Pizza is a hard meal to stretch, and my brothers are like vultures. There are never any leftovers.

I really raced through dinner, but I was finding that I wasn't quite as hungry as usual. Tom had suggested that I eat smaller meals with a snack in between so that I would be more comfortable in the brace. Now I knew what he meant.

I rushed up to call Molly just as Mom announced that she had made my favorite chocolate cake with maple-walnut icing for dessert. Oh, I could just taste it melting in my mouth. It was a favorite of Molly's, too, and she had enjoyed it at many birthdays at our house. She came right over.

As usual, we flopped on my bed and put our chatter on high speed so we could get it all in before Mom called for Molly to go home. I showed Molly the red mark on my tummy and told her I was really having a hard time with the whole brace thing. She just shrugged and stretched her lip so I could see the new brace elastics on her teeth. This was her way of reminding me that we all go through this stuff. I had hoped for a little more sympathy and felt a little disappointed. Molly must have sensed this and asked if she could try my brace on. I was so excited. I wanted to see how it looked on someone else. I fastened the back straps and asked her if she could put my sweatshirt on so that I could *really* see what she looked like. She quickly threw it on. I felt so much better seeing her in it. I could tell, just a tiny bit, that she might have something on underneath the sweatshirt, but it didn't look *that* bad.

We could hear Mom coming up the stairs so I quickly took the brace off Molly. She finished buttoning her blouse just as Mom knocked on the door. We were still giggling when Mom came in. It felt so good to be having fun, even with a brace. Mom explained that I had to get my brace on before cake. Molly asked if she could watch Mom put the brace on. I felt kind of special.

As Mom carefully placed the brace to fit comfortably over my hips, she showed Molly how to fasten it just in case I ever had an emergency at her house and needed to take it off. Mom fastened the bottom strap first, then the middle, and finally the top.

"Molly, you may have to go back and tighten each one to be sure the brace isn't too loose-fitting," said Mom.

Molly watched so seriously.

"Lighten up Molly," I thought. "This is just a brace."

Then we scooted down the stairs to have our cake. I was feeling better.

After Molly left, I went up to the bathroom to brush my teeth and get ready to read. I had very little homework, which meant I could probably finish the book I was reading for my book report. It had taken me a long time to learn how to read, but now I was really on a roll and read every minute I could. If someone had told me in second grade that this would happen, I never would have believed them.

Brace, book, and bed. The routine was just beginning but it was feeling more normal, and I was trying hard to make friends with my new coat of armor. I knew I had to. Molly was my most honest friend, and I had to believe that she was telling the truth: It really didn't look bad. After all, I had seen that for myself.

CHAPTER EIGHT

Tough Skin

The next day in school my tummy felt a little sorer than it had the day before, and my brace felt like it was rubbing against my skin even more. I was very uncomfortable after recess and asked if I could go to Ms. Bennett. Even though Ms. Staples was about to introduce a new math lesson, she seemed to know that this was more important and let me go.

"Maisey, why don't you go on down and check in with Ms. Bennett," said Ms. Staples.

I really liked the way she did things, as if they had been planned the whole time. As I slipped out of my seat, Jean caught my eye and was hoping I could lip read as she stretched her mouth into a big "h" for "how." I knew the rest of the sentence without her even finishing. "How come you're going to the nurse?" is what she was going to say. Ms. Staples, whom we had nicknamed "Antennas" in early October, looked over and gave Jean one of her glares.

When I arrived, Ms. Bennett was on the phone but motioned for me to come in and sit down and quickly hung up.

"Maisey, how are you doing today?"

Before I could get an answer out of my mouth, she went on about how important braces were to creating a positive effect on a curvature and how she knew that this was just an adjustment period. I didn't have the heart to interrupt her so I just sat there and smiled. Finally, she suggested that we take off the brace and have a look.

"Let's take a look at your skin today," said Ms. Bennett.

She gently lifted my undershirt.

"Still looks red, Maisey, but we'll just keep an eye on it."

Unfortunately, I arrived for lunch a bit late and ended up sitting with Charlotte. Charlotte was what my friends and I referred to as a "granola." She eats only health foods, often unwrapping some very interesting-looking lunches. She never takes medicine and pooh-poohs much of what everyone else eats. I knew this would be an interesting meal.

"Hi, Charlotte. Mind if I join you?" I asked.

"No, have a seat," she replied.

As I sat there unwrapping my sandwich, Charlotte just kind of stared at me for a second or two.

"Problem?" I asked.

"No, no, not at all, Maisey. I was wondering, is it true that you're wearing a back brace now?"

"Well, yeah, it is." I answered, feeling a bit invaded. "Why?"

"Maisey, my mom says that people don't need to wear braces to heal their backs. There are other ways to deal with these things."

"I don't believe her," I thought to myself. "Not only is she a granola, but now she's telling me how to heal my body."

I really wanted to just get up and leave. I managed to stay, but only briefly.

I wolfed down my lunch and said good-bye to Charlotte.

I wanted to say, "Good riddance," but I knew better. I was so annoyed. I could see the headlines, "Sugarless Charlotte has new cure for curving backs."

As my mom always says, "It takes all kinds."

Because it had started to rain, lunch recess was very short. Jean was disappointed to hear that I only went to Ms. Bennett to get my brace off. I really don't know what she was hoping for. She headed in with our class while I went to Ms. Bennett. I wanted to share my "Sugarless Charlotte" story with Jean, but I didn't have time.

Ms. Bennett's office was much quieter after lunch. She asked me how lunch was and seemed more chatty than before. I told her about what Charlotte had said and she got quite a chuckle.

"It's not that funny," I thought to myself.

Then she explained that Charlotte was talking about something called "homeopathic medicine" and that there were people who sought other cures or ways to treat problems, more natural ways. I still wasn't quite sure what that meant but it got me thinking.

"Is she right, Ms. Bennett?" I asked.

A big smile spread over her face.

"Absolutely not, Maisey. The only non-surgical method for treating scoliosis is bracing. Your doctor knows exactly what he's doing. You just listen to him and never mind Charlotte."

I felt a little confused, but I'd listen to Ms. Bennett over Charlotte any day. I was still kind of mad at Charlotte for telling me that she knew better. Jean seemed mild compared to Charlotte. Jean would never have said that to me.

Then my thoughts drifted to Molly, my number-one supporter. Molly would study and dissect the whole situation, and then I was sure she would agree that Charlotte was gone, absolutely gone!

As I was finishing up with Ms. Bennett, she explained that she thought my skin was getting slightly more used to the brace.

"Be patient, Maisey. You've only had it a few days."

I didn't exactly agree since my skin was feeling a bit sore in the red areas. But she's the nurse, not me. I thanked her and moved on to my class.

· — ·

I was amazed at how quickly I had fallen into a routine, but I was still pretty unhappy about wearing a brace. I felt very self-conscious and a bit defeated when it came to the boys in my class. A few times one or two of them bumped into me and the expression on their faces was quite revealing. I knew that even though Molly said I looked fine, the kids could really tell that I looked "largely" fine.

The school day was over, and I was back on the bus, excited about going home because my grandparents were coming to visit us from Connecticut. They had just returned from six weeks in Florida, which meant great oranges and lots of hugs and kisses.

My grandfather is the best. He feels like one big, cuddly teddy bear with a scruffy face. He's getting pretty old now, and he always misses half the whiskers on his face when he shaves, and my grandmother never fails to remind him.

"Don't get too close to Granddaddy, Maisey," she warns, "or you'll feel as if someone is using sandpaper on your face!"

Then, the two of them start laughing. At eighty-plus years old, they still have fun together.

As the bus pulled up to the bus stop, I was thrilled to see my welcoming committee of Granddaddy, Grandma, and Mom. The boys were there too because their schools get out earlier than mine. Mark was wearing a shirt that had "Miami Dolphins" across it, and he kept pushing out his chest to show me. Conor was waving a banner that matched Mark's shirt.

"What a circus this scene is!" I thought.

My feet never touched the steps of the bus as I was met with a big hug from Granddaddy, scruffy beard and all.

Grandma was in the background saying, "Walter, her face, her face!"

How I laughed.

As we walked home, Granddaddy made a joke out of my new brace.

"I hear you have on some new protection from your brothers, Maisey!"

Conor and Mark headed over to me as if someone had cued them, and I knew their knuckles were going right at me, but fortunately, Mom intercepted.

Granddaddy went on to say that he thought one of my great-aunts had had scoliosis, but in those days no one did anything about it. Then he mimicked how she had looked as an old woman. I suppose he thought he was helping me out. Mom looked a bit shocked.

Mom explained that the good thing about scoliosis is that you're not really sick, and it doesn't seem to hurt. Even though I hated others speaking for me, after all, it is my back and my scoliosis, Mom was right. It didn't hurt at all. It was a quiet kind of thing that seemed to just sleep in my body . . . at least it seemed to be sleeping.

CHAPTER NINE

Big Doings

For the next five days, there were big doings in our house. Lots of conversation, great walks with Granddaddy, Grandma's homemade desserts, and a schedule that was like one big vacation. Squeezed into all this was school.

Molly came over almost everyday. She became so much a fixture that my brothers even started fighting with her. I knew that Molly loved every minute of it because her house is always so quiet. No one fights with her grandmother over dessert when it's just the two of them. To Molly, being part of our house is the challenge that she misses at home.

A few times over these days I kind of wished I didn't have to wear the brace. I'd be in the middle of a game with Granddaddy, and Mom would announce, "Maisey, time to get back into the brace."

"Go along now, Maisey, and I'll wait here," Granddaddy would say, but I really hated having to stop what was often the best part of the game.

At this point I was able to put the brace on myself. I just needed someone to tighten the straps. If Molly was over, she'd do that for me. She was great about it.

"OK, soldier, here's your bulletproof vest," she would say, and we would both break into laughter.

．￣．

One night Grandma and Granddaddy went to bed very early. Mom and Dad said that we had probably exhausted them. Molly and I sneaked upstairs before Mom could send her home. I hadn't had a chance to tell Molly about my lunch with Charlotte and I really wanted to hear what Molly had to say. After I finished telling her, I was very surprised at her reaction.

"You know, Maisey, I was kind of raised as a 'granola' too. That's why I love it when my grandmother takes care of me because she lets me have things to eat that my mom won't buy. When Mom is home, I am only allowed honey on my cereal, but when Grandma takes care of me she lets me have sugar. Once she even bought me a box of Frosted Flakes, but made me promise not to tell. I had to eat the whole box in four days."

When I really thought about it, Molly is a "granola," and I often avoid eating at her house because the desserts are pretty boring.

"But, Molly, would you tell someone not to wear a brace?" I pleaded.

"No way, Maisey!" Molly replied in an exaggerated tone. "That's where my mom and dad would draw the line. My sister's studying to be a doctor, and her husband is a doctor, and sometimes I hear them talking about the people who refuse surgery and try 'healing' methods of their own. They say that can be very dangerous. When they come to visit, they go on and on about this with my parents. Once my sister's husband was so mad about something that I even heard him use the words 'witch doctor.'"

I was really glad that Molly and I had had time to talk about this. I wasn't as mad when Molly finished, and I understood Charlotte a little better, but I sure didn't agree with her. I certainly did not want to look like my great-aunt when I got old. I was sure that Dr. Bones and Tom wouldn't let me.

"Maisey, Molly, time to call it a night," my mom yelled up the stairs.

"Coming," I called back.

As Molly and I went down the stairs, I could hear my dad talking to my mom for yelling so loudly when my grandparents were asleep. Sometimes it's hard to remember that, when company comes, you have to reorganize a bit.

"I bet Grandma and Granddaddy don't mind," I thought to myself. "They have plenty of time to sleep when they go home."

CHAPTER TEN

Spring Has Sprung, School Is Almost Done

As the daffodils and crocuses began to pop up outside school, so did a lot of conversation inside about spring soccer and a softball team being started for girls. The team would be a first for my school, and it was something I really wanted to do. After years of dodging my brother Mark's "attack" pitches, I had become a pretty good judge of what I could and couldn't hit. One thing I knew for sure: when my bat hit the ball, it went sailing. Not the bat, the ball!

Mark, on the other hand, could hardly hit a ball, which is why he became the family pitcher. Dad used to tell him that he had other strengths but that tasks which involved something called "eye-hand coordination" were challenging for him. That was an understatement! The only reason he got to be the family pitcher was because Dad had us all pull positions out of a hat. I remember how surprised Dad looked when Mark got pitcher. Conor and I weren't surprised, but we were pretty scared . . . of getting hit by his poorly aimed throws.

The best family softball story happened the day we got our new station wagon. Everyone was so excited because we had finally buried the old brown tank that we had before it. Mark

45

was standing in front of the back window of the new car pitching to his friend Frankie. Mom had gone out three times and asked him to move away from the new car. On her way back into the house after her third attempt, there was a huge crash and the unmistakable sound of broken glass. Mark looked like he was in shock as his friend Frankie yelled out, "I think I have to leave now!"

It took the better part of an hour to get all the glass up. I never saw Mark so happy about helping in my life. Later, when Dad was about to walk in the door after work, Mom sent us all upstairs. That was a clue that this was major. We knew she was telling him the news of the day. That was one night that dinner was pretty quiet, and no one hung around for dessert. From then on Mark became the umpire and Mom did the pitching.

. — .

I was scheduled to go see Dr. Bones just before the softball tryouts. It was just a quick brace check to see how things were going. I wanted to ask him about softball, but was a little nervous he might say no. I had been able to do just about anything I wanted so far. I couldn't imagine why he would say no to softball, but I was worried a bit.

Mom had already contacted the coach to see if all the games were in our town or if we would be playing elsewhere. I heard her telling Dad that when she explained to the coach that I had a back brace, the coach got real quiet. I was annoyed that my mom had even called the coach.

"Why couldn't she have just waited?" I thought.

. — .

Things were going along OK in school. I was sure that I would never like wearing the brace, but I knew that it was something I just had to do. Jean was becoming an even better friend, and if anyone asked me how I was doing and Jean was around, she often gave the answer.

"What is this?" I often thought to myself, but I didn't press it. Jean was one person that I always wanted on my side. If she didn't like you, she could be a bit of a meanie.

I really loved our fifth grade because there were a lot of nice kids. Most of us had been together since kindergarten; some of us had even gone to the same preschool. Most of the kids had their own little quirks that we could all laugh about with them, which is better than laughing without them, or at them.

Elizabeth was known as "Elizavoice" because of her deep voice and her ability to keep everyone in stitches. Allison was know as "Bug," which was a nickname her family gave her when she was young and it kind of stuck because her brothers called her that in school. Billy was known as "Hutch" because his last name was Hutchinson. Fred was the "Dipper" because he always had a basketball in his hand, and so on.

Then there were those who didn't have nicknames but had other little things that they were known for. Ivan was famous for his "Twinkies and Gushers." Each morning at snack time he'd wolf down his Twinkies, and then he'd line up all the Gushers on his desk and squeeze them with his fingers. Everyday Ivan would squeeze, hoping that the juice would gush out on his desk rather than in his mouth.

Ms. Staples hated the whole ordeal, and at least once during every snacktime, would say, "Ivan please. Ivan, snack is to be eaten, not played with."

We would all let out a giggle. Ivan loved every minute of it, and it was more like a "snackshow" than "snacktime."

The best was one day when Ivan was really pressing it, and Ms. Staples looked over at him and said in a very loud voice, "Ivan, if those Gushers start gushing, I am going to be very upset."

The principal, Mr. Goodfield, was standing behind her. It was a very funny scene. Ms. Staples turned red as a tomato. School was really as much fun as it was work.

Ms. Bennett was great to me, and I looked forward to our daily check-ins. She knew my schedule by heart and sometimes, if I forgot, she'd call up on the intercom and say, "This is Ms. Bennett. Can you send a messenger down to my office?"

That was our code and Ms. Staples followed it exactly.

She'd look over at me and say, "Maisey, why don't you go down."

No one ever argued or said, "Can't I," so I had a feeling that somehow the kids just knew, and that was OK by me.

One thing that helped a lot was the day Ms. Bennett came into our class and gave her brace presentation. I was amazed at all the things people wore braces for. I was even more amazed that some of my classmates had worn braces themselves: one for a wrist problem and another for hip problems when she was a baby. I even volunteered to show the class my brace the next day. Everybody was really great about it, and, after I showed it to them, I felt much better about wearing it. I wasn't as angry as I was in the beginning.

In addition to the new softball team, one of the highlights of fifth grade is going off to environmental camp. Every fifth grader can go, and we had raised money all year so that everyone could afford the trip. We would be leaving in two weeks, which was another reason why Mom had arranged the appointment with Dr. Bones. She wanted to make sure the brace was fitting properly since I still had one area where it seemed to rub. I wasn't quite as excited about going off to camp now that I had the brace, and I think my mom was hoping that Dr. Bones could help me out with that. When I really stopped to think about it, I kind of wanted to know if I could leave the brace home for the week.

"Why not?" I thought to myself. "After all, I was without it for years so what would be the big deal?"

Dr. Bones's secretary ended up canceling our appointment and rescheduling. That got my mom into a bit of a dither about softball.

"Pat, why don't we just let her try out," encouraged my dad. "We'll explain to Maisey that this is pending approval by Dr. Bones."

Mom agreed with Dad, but I could tell she was still kind of worried about it all. When it comes to anything that has to do with doctors, Mom goes by the book.

· — ·

"Go for it, Maisey! Try to steal to second base, it's a shoo-in," Conor yelled. "Maisey, will you just go for it. What is the matter with you?"

Playing softball with my brothers can be so annoying, but I really needed their help. Conor and Mark are both on teams. Mom and Dad have been taking me to their games for years. From the time the season opens, I spend more dinners on old blankets than I do at our kitchen table. My dream was to be as good at softball as they were at baseball, but the fact of the matter was the only thing I really had down pat was the gum chewing. I could fit four sticks in my mouth at a time and still talk! Mark and Conor could do only three, sometimes three and a half. Even then they spoke like they had marbles in their mouths. For sure, this special talent might impress my teammates, but it would not get me on the girls' softball team.

The day of tryouts it started to sprinkle just as it was my turn up at bat. I kind of felt that they had saved the worst for last. It was no secret in my house that I am afraid of thunder and lightning.

So just as I was about to swing my bat, Mark yelled out, "Maisey, the lightning is coming!"

I let go and swung that bat as if the lightning was about to attack me.

The ball sailed over second base with Conor screaming, "Steal, Maisey, steal for home."

I ran so fast I felt like my legs weren't even attached to my body.

As I slid into home plate the umpire yelled, "Everybody off the field!"

Just as we shut the car door a huge bold of lightning came, followed by a crack of thunder that could have broken the sound barrier. It was very scary.

Three days later I got the call. I had made the team. From that day on, I had a whole new outlook on thunderstorms as well as older brothers!

· — ·

Two days after I made the team, Mom and I once again traveled into the city to see Dr. Bones. We had the check-in down pat and before long we were in one of the patient rooms waiting for Dr. Bones. Just before he came in, Mom took out a paper covered with writing.

"My question sheet, Maisey. Don't worry, it's not as long as it might look," she assured me.

"Oh no," I thought. "Here we go again."

Before I got a chance to comment, there was a knock at the door and in walked Dr. Bones.

"Maisey, Mrs. MacGuire, nice to see you again."

Dr. Bones greeted us like an old friend, and I must admit, I kind of got excited about seeing him again. This time he offered to help me out of my brace himself, which I really did not mind at all. I had my special undershirt on to protect my skin, and I knew it would be faster.

"Maisey, how is the brace feeling to you now that you've had it on for a few months? Any concerns, complaints?"

I carefully lifted my shirt and showed him the pressure marks under my arms and the ones just below the brace across my tummy. He agreed that it looked a bit tender and suggested some cornstarch and, when it got better, some alcohol to toughen my skin. As he was finishing, Tom arrived to get some direction from Dr. Bones about adjusting my brace. Tom explained that he could fix it by heating the bottom and pushing it out a bit.

The whole time they were talking I had my own agenda. I kept hoping that each of them would ask me what was new so that I could report about making the team.

My mom read my mind and said, "You both should ask Maisey about her big news."

As embarrassed as I was, I couldn't wait to tell.

"I made the girls' softball team," I blurted out as they both gave a great big belly laugh.

"Maisey, that's great. Congratulations!" responded Dr. Bones.

"Give me five," added Tom as he put his hand out.

"Now remember, Maisey," Dr. Bones added. "You can save your out-of-brace time for practice and games, but be sure to monitor the time carefully. Those games can get pretty long, so on the days that you have games, you may want to keep your brace on until it's time for the first pitch."

I was relieved that Dr. Bones didn't tell me I couldn't play but not very happy about his warning regarding my out-of-brace time. From the very beginning he had said that I could do most of the things I had done before I got the brace, but I still needed to hear it again. I had been so upset about wearing the brace that I guess I hadn't completely listened to what he said at our last appointment.

Then Mom added her two cents, "Since we're talking about activities . . . Maisey is off to environmental camp next week, Dr. Bones, and I was wondering if there is anything we need to know?"

"Oh no," I thought to myself. "Mom's back on her list again!"

"Just the usual. Watch the time out of the brace. Maisey, let your teachers know if your brace is uncomfortable in any way. No swimming in the brace or getting it wet. And whatever you do, don't let any of your friends convince you to let them wear it for a day."

And with that everyone burst out laughing. Somehow I didn't find it quite that funny, and I thought it was kind of a weird thing to say.

"Who would want to borrow this?" I thought to myself.

Mom and I waited in the patient room while Tom took the brace to the casting room to make the necessary adjustments. Dr. Bones wished me well on all my adventures and just as he was closing the door he called out, "Don't forget to hit a grand slam for me, Maisey."

He made it all seem so normal, having a brace that is. As much as I hated wearing it, Dr. Bones and Tom really listened to all my complaints and seemed to understand.

Tom returned in a few minutes and placed the brace gently on my body. The bottom edge was still warm. It felt much more comfortable, especially under my left arm, which had been rubbing quite a bit. I am left-handed and found myself raising my hand less and less in class because it was so uncomfortable. I hadn't said too much about it, but now I could really feel the difference.

We thanked Tom and as we said good-bye he gave me one last reminder. "Now, Maisey, next time you have a mark from the brace that is uncomfortable, you need to come in right away so that you don't get a pressure sore."

Tom was right. I really should have told the nurse and my mom how uncomfortable I had been. It had gotten a lot worse, and I really was kind of silly not to tell. Little by little, I was learning more and more.

CHAPTER ELEVEN

Off to Journey's End

"Maisey, I am so jealous," groaned Molly. "My school only offers day trips. I would love to go to environmental camp. It would be so neat."

Molly had come over to help me pack. We were wondering how we would survive not talking for five days. She was even more excited than me about my trip to "Journey's End." Personally, I thought it was kind of an unusual name for an environmental camp. It sounded like I might not come back. The camp is located about two hours away. When Mark went, he reported seeing a black bear on a night walk. Conor didn't believe him and said that Mark was such a wimp that he never would have gotten that close to anything that moved in the dark to know it was a bear. Normally, if you catch Mark in a lie, he will argue and argue to convince you it's the truth. When Conor accused him of lying about the black bear, Mark just shrugged his shoulders and walked away.

"Just maybe it's the truth," I thought to myself.

. — .

"Maisey, I can't believe how many pairs of sweatpants you're bringing. I don't even own one pair," said Molly.

"Well, neither did I until I got the brace," I snapped back.

I didn't mean to be so sharp, but she kind of hurt my feelings. I hated the sweatpants but I had no other choice with the brace, at least not for tramping in the woods. My jeans tend to rub when I walk long distances. Sweatpants are the most comfortable.

"Maisey, I'm sorry. I just wasn't thinking," replied Molly.

Molly is so great. We always work things out. She's a lot like me: sensitive, caring, loves to laugh, and really likes having fun. Just as she was about to help me run down my list for the last time, Mom called up the stairs and said it was time for Dad to walk her home.

"Molly, here's my address. Promise me that you'll write."

"OK, Maisey, but you're only going to be there for four nights. You may only get one letter."

"That's fine, Molly. One will be great. I'll write you back, I promise," I said.

After Molly left, Mom came up to see how I was doing.

"How's my girl? All packed? I'm here to help if you have more to do."

Mom is great and always makes an adventure extra special. I'm sure she knew that I could never get everything done when Molly was over because we talk too much.

Mom helped me finish up the very last of my packing by going over the checklist with me and then spent a few minutes reviewing my brace schedule. In the morning she would show Ms. Staples and two of the other fifth-grade teachers how to put my brace on.

"I know you may not like it, Maisey, but they need to know how to help you get in and out of it," Mom said.

She was right and I knew it, but it was still not the greatest. I worried that someone might come into the nurse's office while Mom was showing them.

"Maisey, I'm really proud of you. You have done so well with your brace, and you have made such a wonderful adjustment. I know this has not been easy for you," she said.

Even though I hadn't given it much thought, I guess I had adjusted well, at least most of the time. The fact of the matter is, I felt that I looked inflated in the brace, and I still hated it when I bumped into one of the boys. They were wicked.

"Go, Maisey," they yelled.

It really made me mad. But the brace wasn't that big a deal. Well, sometimes it was, but there wasn't much I could do about it.

. — .

Going to sleep that night was a real challenge. I was so excited, and I had butterflies in my tummy, dive-bombing and having a grand old time. How could I ever get them to understand that I really needed my sleep?

"Mai . . . sey, time to get up. I have a piece of French toast with your name on it," called my mom.

Just as Mom finished her sentence, my dad tapped on my door, "Come on, Lazy Maisey, time to rise and shine."

As I dragged myself into the bathroom, I felt as if I hadn't slept a wink. The butterflies were finally in a dead sleep, and the rest of my body wanted to join them.

Conor and Mark were almost done when I arrived at the table.

"The camp food is going to be lousy," commented Mark.

"The showers are sometimes cold," chimed in Conor.

"Boys, that's enough," scolded Mom. "Go along and get yourselves off to school. The bus will be here in ten minutes."

I was so tired that their comments didn't even bother me. I just wanted a warm bed and a dark room, but I knew I'd feel differently once I got to school.

While I was dressing, Dad carried my bags downstairs while Mom packed a snack for the bus ride.

. — .

As we pulled up to the school parking lot, all you could see were cars with students and parents unloading suitcases, duffle bags, sleeping bags, and pillows. It would have made such a funny picture for a camp ad. Mom carried my bag and I wondered if she had taken energy pills when I saw how quickly she moved. She was definitely on a mission. It didn't take long for me to understand why. As I waited in line for one last health check from the school nurse, Mom gathered up Ms. Staples and the two other female fifth-grade teachers to show them how to do my brace. As they approached the nurse's line, Ms. Bennett called me to the front so that I could go off with the teachers. My mother probably knew how embarrassed I was, but there was no other way to do this. It absolutely had to be done quickly since all the parents were looking for the teachers to ask them last-minute questions.

We sneaked into the nurse's office and closed the door. Ms. Staples agreed to go last and guard the door. I appreciated her sensitivity. I quickly removed my shirt, and Mom stood behind me explaining how the brace needed to be placed on my body.

"As you place the brace on Maisey's body, be sure it rests comfortably on her hips. First you fasten the bottom or middle strap to be sure that it is stabilized on her pelvic area. You don't want to compress her ribs and you want to be sure that the brace is not too loose-fitting. After you do the last strap, which will be the top strap, you may need to go back and tighten the middle and bottom straps a bit more. The most important thing is to be sure it fits tightly but comfortably. If a brace is too loose it is the same as a shoe that is too big," explained Mom.

Then Ms. Staples left her post guarding the door and offered to try to put the brace on me. She was both gentle and confident, and I could feel my relief as she finished up. As the teachers rushed out the door to gather their classes for the final check, I quickly put on my topshirt and gave my mom a huge hug. She really was the best, and I knew it.

I sat with Jean and Elizavoice on the bus, and we had such a good time that the ride seemed like it was over in just minutes. They were also going to be my bunkmates, so I knew I was in for a great week. My friends Kyanna and Gina would be in the room next door to us. It had worked out perfectly. Elizavoice has asthma and would be going to the nurse each day for her medication, so I felt very comfortable about everything.

. — .

As the buses pulled up to Journey's End, I was speechless. It looked really, really rustic. The camp was way out in the country and right in front of the camp was a huge lake, which seemed to shimmer from the sun's rays. The main house, where we would be having meals, had a huge deck on it overlooking the lake. The meeting room, which was on the back side of the main house, was full of stuffed animals that had once been alive. The individual cottage units were located all around the main house but farther back into the woods. Each cabin had a bathroom and eight bunkrooms with at least two bunks in each of them. In the middle was a common area called the activity room. The boys' cottages were on one side of the woods and the girls' cottages on the other.

Each cottage had at least one teacher and one staff member from Journey's End. Each morning we were expected to be up and in the dining-hall area of the main house by seven forty-five for breakfast. Lunch was at noon sharp, and dinner at five thirty. All the meals were family style, so if you didn't like something, you didn't have to eat it. The counselors reminded us, however, that there would be some pressure to be at a table without waste since it was an environmental camp. Their motto was, "If you take it, you eat it."

After we unloaded our bags from the buses, we were sent into the meeting room of the main house to get our cottage assignments. My cottage was called "Morning Star," and a plaque on the front told the story of this Native American name. Each cottage had its own name and plaque. We quickly threw our bags in our room and set off for the main house for lunch.

"The counselors are so organized," I thought to myself, and they looked like they just loved having us.

In the dining hall each cottage had its own table with meal duties assigned to each camper. Lunch was excellent, grilled cheese, fruit cup, brownies, and fresh fruit to take for an afternoon snack.

After lunch we went back into the meeting room. The counselors were very entertaining and asked us to think about some of the things that we might be doing at Journey's End. After the brainstorming, they explained what we might find on the two hundred acres of land that the camp occupied.

The activity list was wonderful: hunting animal tracks; building animal shelters out of natural materials from the woods; scavenger hunts looking for signs of spring; migrant birds; planting a children's garden; ponding; making tea out of mint grown in the woods; and best of all, star gazing and night walks.

Every time the counselor mentioned a new activity, Elizavoice yelled out, "Cool, definitely something I want to do."

Then the whole group went into a giggle, even our teachers. Our counselor explained that at night we would gather in the activity rooms of our individual cottages to hear Native American stories.

· — ·

Our counselor was Mariel; her nickname was M-rail, but I had no idea why. She had curly hair tied up into short, stubby braids and wore an old work shirt and a pair of jeans that had been patched so much that they looked more like a patchwork quilt. She made everything we did so much fun.

Each day at camp seemed to fly by. Molly came through with a letter and a funny card and even my brothers managed to write. (I knew my mom arranged that.) M-rail wrote postcards to the kids who didn't get mail and sneaked them into the mailbag. I knew it was her doing because I saw her sorting through the mail one afternoon with the postcards at her side. This camp seemed to care about kids in every way.

The most exciting thing happened one night when we lost power. We were having a heavy thunderstorm with lots of lightning. At dinner they told us that if we had a flashlight, we might want to get it out. You could tell everyone was a bit nervous. At about eight thirty, when I was brushing my teeth in the girls' bathroom, there was a huge crack of lightning and suddenly, everything went black.

Elizavoice, who was standing next to me, grabbed my arm and in the quietest voice I have ever heard, whispered, "Maisey, I'm scared."

I was pretty scared myself and very relieved when Ms. Staples appeared with her flashlight in hand. She helped us back to our bunkroom.

When we got there, Bug was sitting on her bunk holding a flashlight and whining, "I told you guys to hurry up."

That night most of us ended up sleeping in one room, many of us on the floor. Can you blame us?

. — .

Of all the activities, I liked our night walk the best. M-rail gave each of us a flashlight but at certain times told us to turn it off and just think about night vision and what it's like for the animals. We went into the wetlands way back behind the cabins and looked at the outlines of the trees, which were reflected off the little pond by a big, round, perfect ball of a moon. Elizavoice was speechless and Bug was so moved that she began to cry. Even the skunk cabbage looked different and our counselor told us how the Native Americans used it long ago for baby diapers because it absorbs moisture. As we quietly stood there looking at the shapes of the trees in the night and listening to the sounds, it was as eerie as it was moving. My brace seemed so unimportant, and I felt like I was a colonist and had just come to the New World.

On the way back, as we approached the cottages, we could see a rather woolly figure on the back side of the cottage next to ours. M-rail made us stop dead in our tracks and told us not to make a peep. Sure enough it was a black bear and he seemed to be looking for something. As he headed back toward the woods, M-rail scooted us onto the path that led to our cabin. You never saw a group move so quickly in your whole life, and Ms. Staples, not far from retirement, was in the lead. When we got into our cabin, she looked as white as the hair on her head.

I couldn't wait to go home and tell Mark about it. I knew that he had been telling the truth about his own camp experience even though Conor had doubted him. This would make for an excellent story, even if Conor didn't believe me.

I wanted camp to last forever, and it was hard to believe how quickly the time went by. I had gotten mail everyday. Four different people had done my brace with no problems except a mosquito bite that was a bit itchy one night. I had also learned a lot about the Native Americans. Most of all, I loved rooming and camping with my friends.

Just before we said good-bye to M-rail, she explained her nickname to us. She had taken a year off from college and traveled by train all over the United States. She ended up at Journey's End when she ran out of money and so they hired her and nicknamed her M-rail.

The night the mosquito bit me under my brace she got up with me, took my brace off, put some calamine lotion on the bite, and explained that her brother had a leg brace. She told me all the neat things he had been able to do, even with the brace.

"Attitude, Maisey, that's the secret. If you have a good positive attitude, you'll do fine. Don't ever forget that."

As we were leaving, M-rail gave each of us a big hug, and I hugged her back as hard as I could.

"I won't forget what you said, M-rail. Never."

As I went up the stairs of the bus, Jean, Jean, the Gossip Queen was already starting, but somehow I kind of enjoyed her instant replay of the cabin stories. It was like having an oral newspaper, and I knew it would make the ride home an enjoyable one.

CHAPTER TWELVE

School's Done, Summer Fun

The last few weeks of school were jam-packed with activities. We were the last fifth grade that would ever be in our school, since they had reorganized the grades and would now be putting the fifth graders in the middle school. The last big event was the Parent Breakfast. We had an assembly of fifth graders, parents, and teachers at which each class read a list of things that fifth grade had meant to them. When they got to Ms. Staples's class, Jean and I read the list. As we finished the last comment, which was "Little Friends, Big Friends," I quietly said to myself "and a back brace." The microphone I was using picked it up. Everybody started to laugh. I was so embarrassed that I quickly handed the microphone to Mr. Goodfield and sat down. I just couldn't believe I had done that. For once, even Jean was in shock. My mom and dad just smiled. I think they knew how I felt.

After the assembly, all the fifth-grade students and teachers went over to the recreation department's indoor pool and had a picnic and swim party. Even Ms. Staples got in the pool. She was so much fun and participated in all our water games. I knew I was really going to miss her.

When I had first found out about the pool party, I was very nervous about how I would work out my brace time the day of the swim since I also had softball practice. As it turned out, I did use up most of my time, so I ended up having to go to softball practice in my brace. The coach looked really nervous, but for me it was better than missing it altogether.

Each time the coach looked over at me, I wanted to go over to her and say, "Cool your jets, please; you're wearing glasses." But I didn't, and it really did work out OK. Sometimes people can have such hang-ups.

· — ·

On the very last day of school, I felt so weird when I woke up. Molly even called to wish me luck. Her school goes all the way up to high school, so she wouldn't experience these endings until later. I'm not sure who was more emotional, my mom or me. My mom had been very active in the school and besides, she always gets teary about our transitions.

Mom offered to drive me to school, but I didn't want to miss the last day with Mr. Barrett, our bus driver. He was retiring from driving and had been my driver since kindergarten. He was kind of like a grandfather to all of the "busers," as we called ourselves. He really cared about us, and he was a very good driver, especially when the weather was bad.

When we got to school we saw Mr. Goodfield in the middle of the hallway greeting all of us as we headed up the stairs or down the hall to our classrooms. His first name is Alvin, which we used to kind of make fun of, but I realized what a great name Alvin really is and most of all, what a great principal he had been. I remembered how kind he was to me the very first day I wore my brace to school. He gave me a little smile as I was leaving the nurse's office that day and said, "Maisey, you're going to do just fine because we're here to help you."

At the time, it didn't seem like such a big deal, but it really did mean a lot to me.

When I got to my classroom door, I burst out laughing. Ms. Staples was standing there with a curly blond wig on and a big smile. She always used to tell us that at one time in her life she had been a blond. Somehow, we never really believed her. This was her way of letting us see how she had looked. It was really very, very funny because it was not like her at all to do such a wild thing.

The day flew by and we spent most of our time counting books and cleaning out our desks. Since it was boiling outside, we even got double recess and Popsicles. Ms. Bennett called up right before lunch so I could go down and take my brace off. My undershirt was soaking wet, so I put on a fresh one. Boy, wearing this thing in the heat of the summer was not going to be fun.

When I went back after lunch, Ms. Bennett gave me a tiny little china butterfly sitting on a leaf. My mom had baked something for her, and I knew Ms. Bennett would love it. She promised me that it was going to be just as easy at the middle school, but I was not so sure. It was a much bigger school, with kids from all over town. I didn't want the nurse to do a brace talk there. Hopefully, the fact that my brother Mark would also be there would make it easier.

Before I knew it, we were all hugging and saying our good-byes.

"Maisey, if there's any hot news you think I should know be sure to write to me at camp. Remember, tell me first," screamed Jean as she headed for her bus.

"Call me and give me your camp address," I yelled back.

Grammar school had ended, and I was about to begin a whole new chapter in my life. Except for the brace, I knew I would just love it. Best of all, I sure was going to enjoy my summer break.

CHAPTER THIRTEEN

Downtime

Whoever invented summer really knew what they were doing. Having some downtime from the rush, rush, rush of school days is so great. I planned to spend the first two weeks sleeping late, lying around, and sitting in front of the TV. But I had so much to do. I wanted to go to the library to sign up for the Great Books Summer Reading Program. I also wanted to get to the things in my bedroom that I never seem to see during the school year. I especially love going through my picture albums, my treasures. I add to them each summer. I have one of those inexpensive instant cameras. I take it with me everywhere. I think I got that from my mom because she is always snapping pictures and has great piles of albums. Sometimes the people are missing heads or feet, but we usually know who they are!

The first few weeks I was planning to spend a lot of time with Molly since she wouldn't be going off to overnight camp until the Fourth of July weekend. I hated that she would be gone for eight weeks. Her camp is way up in New York State, and she only gets one visit from her parents during her whole stay. I don't think I would like that. I'd be so afraid that I was missing out on something at home. Besides, going back to a routine for eight weeks of summer sure doesn't sound like downtime to me. But Molly always reminds me how much she likes camp and how neat it is to have friends from all over the country.

I began getting ready to go away myself for my annual visit to my grandparents in Westport, Connecticut. They live by the shore, and I love to get up each morning and walk down to the beach with my grandfather. I know lots of kids there: some are from Westport and others are what my grandfather calls "transplants," the summer renters. My favorite time is after dinner when all the kids meet at the beach gate and set up teams to play hide-and-seek. It's so much fun. I know all the best hiding places because my grandfather showed them to me. He said he used to hide himself. My grandmother says that no hiding place can be that old!

Most summers my grandparents drive up to get me and then I drive back with them. This time Mom would be going along and staying a night or two before heading back home. I knew she was doing it because of my brace, even though she made up some other excuse. The boys would stay home with Dad: Conor would be working on his water safety certificate for becoming a lifeguard, and Mark would be attending a tennis program. One of our neighbors would cover for Mom during the day.

· ⌐ ·

I couldn't believe how fast the time went. Molly and I had breakfast together almost every morning and overnights nearly every other day. A sure sign that Molly's parents are away is when Molly announces that she has a box of Frosted Flakes. I even saw her grandmother eating them. Can you imagine, a rebellious grandmother?

Soon it was July 1, and Molly and I were going over our lists for our trips. Molly's was like a short story, while mine was just a lot of undershirts, swimsuits, shorts, and tops. When we finished, we were going to just hang out in my room. Molly seemed to be in one of her deep moods.

"Maisey, I can't believe that you are going off to the beach for two weeks and you haven't even mentioned your brace once. You are amazing," she said.

Suddenly, I felt this shock go through my body.

"My brace," I thought to myself. "How am I ever going to be able to hang out at the beach most of the day and part of the evening with a brace?"

"Yikes, Molly, I never even thought about my brace. What am I going to do? I don't want kids I hardly know seeing me in a brace. It's never going to be the same. I'm going to be embarrassed. I'm not even sure I want to go now. This brace is such a pain."

Molly felt so bad that she had even mentioned it, but I was happy she did. This was something that I really needed to work out before I went. I knew Molly couldn't really help me with this. I needed to talk to my mom. I could feel those butterflies surfing in my stomach again.

Molly seemed to know that I was distracted. She kept apologizing, but I really felt she had saved the day. Leave it to Molly to process what I should have thought about myself. I guess I was so excited about being out of school that I just hadn't thought ahead. Actually, I did think about the brace a little because I suspected Mom was driving me down to Connecticut because of it, but I just never let my mind take that next step. Oh, how I wish I had.

After Molly left, I stayed in my room for what seemed like forever. I was so frustrated and so angry that this clunky brace was going to ruin my trip.

"Maisey, it's Mom. Can I come in?"

I knew just by the way she was asking that Molly must have said something to her.

"OK," I replied.

"You know, Maisey, we haven't had one of our 'chew the fat' sessions in a while."

I hated it when my mom used those ancient terms. Why couldn't she be normal and say "Let's talk."

It didn't take me long to let out how bummed I was about the beach and my brace. My mom could see that I was pretty freaked out about the whole thing. She just lay there for a while and listened as I went through a normal day at the beach.

When I finally got it all out, she just kind of smiled and said, "Maisey, I gave Shelley Proctor's mom a call the other day. (Shelley is a beach friend who lives right next to the beach gate.) I explained to her that you now have a brace. Her mom is a nurse and knows all about back braces. Granddaddy reminded me of this when I called him to firm up your stay. Mrs. Proctor has volunteered to help you with it, so you don't have to leave the beach each day and go up to Grandma and Granddaddy's."

At first, I was a little uncomfortable about it all, but Mom was pretty convincing. Ms. Proctor is one of the nicest moms at the beach, and Shelley is my beach version of Molly, so I kind of knew it might work out. I sure didn't want to spend my whole summer home with my brothers. And besides, Girl Scout camp was coming up, too, and I needed to work this whole brace thing out.

Mom and I "hashed" it out (Oh, no, I'm picking up her old-fashioned sayings!) a bit more, and then it was time to say good night. I figured if I slept on it, I might feel better about it. I sure hoped so.

The next day, while Mom baked for what seemed like hours, I finished up my packing and walked down to the library for a new book. The boys were being particularly annoying since their activities hadn't begun yet, and none of us was used to being together twenty-four hours a day. Mom got so fed up with us that she made bubble water and gave us bubble sticks for the yard to give her a break. Within minutes we seemed to have the whole neighborhood around with these huge bubbles filling the sky, and the littler kids running around trying to pop them. It was one chaotic scene. Mom was so busy going in and out that she almost burned the bread she was baking for my grandparents.

Fortunately, our neighbor was taking my brothers to a Red Sox game so dinner would be fairly calm. It would be kind of a treat to be alone with my parents. Mom and I would be leaving for Connecticut in the morning, and Dad would be on deck with the boys, which is always pretty funny. Mom always leaves him these long, long lists, which he goes over and over with her.

. — .

We weren't even out of the driveway ten minutes when Dad called on her car phone to clarify one last thing. Parents can be so predictable.

The drive to Westport was OK and at times kind of boring. We always go through this long tunnel about an hour before my grandparents' house, so I know when the tunnel is behind us that we are two-thirds of the way there. As we pulled up to Grandma and Granddaddy's, Mom started tooting the horn and out they came. They just love to see us. Grandma always has her apron on so I know there are treats inside.

While we unloaded the car, everyone seemed to be talking at once. Granddaddy gave me a big hug and quietly asked me how the "armor" was working out. That was his way of letting me know that they were all set for me. After a great lunch and a lot of talk, Mom and I took a walk down to the beach. I knew we were probably going to end up at Shelley's house even though Mom didn't say so.

We were hardly out of my grandparents' driveway when I could smell the salt air. In five minutes I was looking at Old Mill Beach and Long Island Sound. Ken's Candy Store was still there, always in need of repair, and the same faces began to pass us as we entered the gate to the beach. I didn't recognize the guard at the gate who checked the beach stickers. He was new.

Shelley's mom was out in her garden and came running over, hollering to Shelley, who was inside. Mrs. Proctor gave me a huge hug, which made me feel especially good this time. While Mom and Mrs. Proctor talked, Shelley and I walked along the beach catching up on the past year. We never seem to get around to writing to each other, so there is always lots to talk about. It didn't take long before we got to my brace. Shelley didn't seem to be that surprised about it and explained that she had friends from school who were either in back braces themselves or knew relatives who had scoliosis.

"Maisey, it's not that big a deal. You're going to be so amazed at how quickly the time goes by and at how great your back is when it's over," she said.

I wanted to ask her if any of them had to have surgery, but I was afraid of what the answer might be. We headed back to the house and decided to change into our bathing suits for a quick swim or "dip," as the beach crowd calls it.

Mrs. Proctor seemed to know just how to take my brace off and put it back on. Mom was right. I was excited that with their house right at the beach, I could put it on and take it off as needed. Mrs. Proctor didn't seem to mind at all. She even knew that I might need extra undershirts on really hot days.

After the swim Mom and I headed back to my grandparents so that they didn't feel we had abandoned them. I kind of wanted to stay at the beach but that would have been a rude thing to do on the very first day.

Before dinner Mom gave Grandma a brace lesson. My grandmother seemed a bit nervous about doing it correctly and her hands had trouble holding the brace open. Her arthritis seemed to be getting worse. Mom suggested that maybe it would be easier for Granddaddy to do, but my grandmother wouldn't hear of it.

Mom stayed for part of the next day and then headed home. Because she left so late, I didn't get a lot of time at the beach, which disappointed me. I was thrilled when Granddad suggested he walk me down after dinner so I could play hide-and-seek. He even remembered that I could take my brace off for two more hours.

． ― ．

Each day at my grandparents' was better than the one before and I really hated the thought of leaving them. Other than two very hot days, my brace worked out and, although I longed to be out of it, I managed to get my swimming in as well as my sunbathing. Most evenings I had to put it back on for the hide-and-seek games and some evenings I was so pooped from the sun that I passed on the after-dinner activities.

Shelley's mom was wonderful and each time she took the brace on or off me she shared a tidbit or two about scoliosis. As it turned out, part of her job is to go into the schools in Westport and help with screening the fifth graders. More and more I realized that I was not alone with this thing but I still kept wondering "Why me?"

My grandparents decided to drive me home. Although I love them dearly, I knew it would make the trip twice as long. My grandfather hardly puts the pedal to the metal. Sometimes when he drives, there are lines and lines of cars behind us, people yelling out their windows or making gestures that my grandmother calls "sinful."

No matter what they do, my grandmother always says, "Maisey, they are just having a bad day."

Somehow I have the feeling that my grandfather is making that bad day worse. After I got home, I went up and unpacked and read three wonderful letters, from Jean, Molly, and Elizavoice, all of whom I missed.

My grandparents stayed with us for about three days. They always drive back on Monday to avoid traffic. I think my grandfather knows he is annoying the other drivers. Dad said that we probably wouldn't see them again until fall. The trip to our house is pretty major for two people in their eighties.

For the next week I took it easy. We went to the town recreation area, did some swimming, and I relaxed with the neighborhood kids. I especially missed Molly. My brothers were more manageable and at night we often played kickball or tag. The brace made it a bit harder for me to run as fast as before so I never seemed to win. Conor reminded me that I didn't win without the brace either.

CHAPTER FOURTEEN

Second Chances

With my grandparents' visit over, I began getting a little nervous about Girl Scout camp. I didn't know anyone who was going but I wanted to go anyway. Everyone says it's a great camp, and it's located right on a huge lake. The boys' camp is on the other side. My mom called the camp, and there would be another girl there with a brace, so that made me feel better. Still, I was a little nervous. I would have to walk through the woods to the nurse each time I needed to get the brace taken on or off.

Camp day arrived, and we all piled into the car and drove to Sandwich, which is right over the Bourne Bridge on the edge of Cape Cod. It was a real family affair: Conor and Mark came too. It was about 90°, and the car was packed full of all my camp stuff. Traffic seemed to be backed up for miles. I could just feel the sweat dripping under my brace. I felt like a soggy, stuffed pig.

We were late arriving at camp, which probably meant that I would get my bunk last. As we were unpacking the car, I could hear a voice calling.

"Oh, no," I thought to myself. "This can't be 'Sugarless Charlotte.'"

Before I got a chance to be sure, Charlotte was standing in front of me with her parents in tow, announcing that she had saved me the bottom bunk because of my brace. I was horrified. Her mother explained to my parents that she had called the camp to see if there was anyone that Charlotte might know. When they said my name, that was it. Charlotte had found her bunkmate. I, on the other hand, was ready to repack and leave.

Charlotte never stopped talking from the car to the cabin, and I longed for earplugs to shut her out. My brothers kept rolling their eyes as if to say, "Good luck to you, Maisey!" My parents looked relieved, which really annoyed me.

"Why isn't anyone getting it?" I thought to myself.

For once my brothers seemed to be the only ones who understood my predicament.

· ― ·

When we got to the cabin, the other two girls seemed very nice and a bit overwhelmed by Charlotte.

"I hope they don't think I'm like that, too," I thought.

Charlotte announced to my parents that she could help me get organized.

"She's going to drive me crazy," I said under my breath.

Finally, my mom got the message and off we went to the nurse.

The nurse was OK. Not as nice as Ms. Proctor and Ms. Bennett, though. She suggested that I find a bunkmate to help me with the brace to save me the trip to her office. My mom agreed that would be easier and suggested that I talk to Charlotte. Before I could give my opinion, the nurse said she would take care of that and it was a done deal. I was so annoyed at everyone.

My mom picked up my vibes and said, "Maisey, use your head about this. Charlotte at least knows you, and she really wants to help. This is working out much better than I expected."

I started to describe the cafeteria experience with Charlotte but before I knew it, Charlotte was standing there, and I wasn't able to finish.

As we said our good-byes to our parents, Charlotte looked like she had found her "manitou," me! I was completely freaked out. This is not what I was expecting at all, and I had two whole weeks of it ahead of me.

When we got back to the cabin, I began to organize while Charlotte just sat on the upper bunk watching me. Flora and Carla, our other roommates, had been to the camp before and were talking about who had come back this year and who had not. They really seemed to know everything about the camp.

I looked up at Charlotte at one point, and she was giving me a funny look, rolling her eyes as if to say, "I guess we're the rookies." It was pretty funny.

A counselor named Mindy soon arrived and announced that she was our "in-charge person" and would be checking in with us throughout each day. She knew Flora and Carla and told Charlotte and me that we were in good company. I guess that meant they were OK.

Pretty soon there was a clang, and it was time for lunch. Flora and Carla went ahead while Charlotte and I tried to figure out the direction of the mess hall, which was what they called the room where we ate. My dad, who had been in the Navy, loved the name "mess hall" and said it reminded him of the his old Navy days. Why are parents always reliving their past? Beats me.

Mindy was in charge of three cabins and we all sat at this big, long table and ate family style. It reminded me of Journey's End. Charlotte saved me a seat while I stood in line forever, waiting for my chocolate milk. With the exception of the chocolate milk, Charlotte and I had the exact same lunch on our trays. We had both passed on the hot dogs, which Charlotte whispered might really be chopped-up dogs' tails. The grilled cheese was much more to our liking. Although I expected Charlotte to comment on my chocolate milk, she didn't. As much as I hated to admit it, I was relieved that she was there.

After lunch we had a gathering of campers, and we all said where we were from and whether we had ever been to overnight camp before. First the counselors started it off and then we followed. It was interesting hearing where everyone was from. Some had come quite a distance. I couldn't wait to write and tell Molly. After we introduced ourselves, the counselors ran through our daily schedule. It sounded somewhat like environmental camp with the addition of swimming as well as some co-ed evening socials with the boys across the lake. Charlotte didn't seem too excited about that part but I was until I realized I might have my brace on.

"Oh how embarrassing that will be," I thought.

After our group chat, it was time for swimming. Just as we were leaving for our cabins, the nurse approached Charlotte and me.

Before I could say a word, Charlotte said, "Hey, Maisey, if you want I'll help with your brace."

Then the nurse made the request to Charlotte, and she almost forgot I was even there.

"Ms. Bennett would have done this better," I thought.

Charlotte was very willing to have a brace lesson and so she and I followed the nurse back to the infirmary. I was impressed with how serious and careful Charlotte was about this task. She was almost as good as Molly; in all fairness, she was the same.

As we were racing back to our cabin, Charlotte grabbed my arm and said, "Don't worry, Maisey. I won't ever say a word to anyone about your brace."

She looked like she really meant it.

"Thanks, Charlotte. I'm really glad you're here."

I couldn't believe the words came out of my mouth and you know what, I really was glad.

Swimming in a lake after being in the ocean is pretty weird. Instead of seeing the horizon, I saw the cabins to the boys' camp and a bunch of crazy boys all looking over the water and laughing at us. Charlotte looked over a few times and commented on what jerks boys were. It was pretty obvious that she didn't have any brothers.

After swimming we barely had enough time to get dressed before dinner. Charlotte was really great about rushing so that we could head on down to the nurse's cabin to get my brace. By the time we got to dinner, things were pretty picked over, and we had to sit in two different places. I felt kind of bad, but Charlotte was really a good sport.

When it was finally time to go to bed, I realized that there was no way I could dress in such a tiny cabin without Flora and Carla seeing my brace. Hard as I tried, it was pretty obvious that there was more than just me in my clothes.

Carla was the first to notice.

"Maisey, I didn't know you had a brace. You must have scoliosis like my cousin Michelle."

Then Flora started, "Oh, I'd love to see what your brace looks like because one of my friends in school is getting one, too."

Before I had a chance to answer, Charlotte had become Jean, Jean, the Gossip Queen, and began answering for me. We ended up spending the whole night sitting on our bunks talking about our bodies. I think we actually talked ourselves to sleep, because the next thing I remember was Mindy trying to wake us up.

· — ·

I don't know where the days went, but before I knew it, we were sitting around a campfire singing our good-bye song. Before the song, unit awards were given out, and I was so proud when they called Charlotte's name. At first, she just sat there as if she didn't hear them call her name. Finally, Flora and I gave her a push, and she went up to receive her award. When Mindy finished making her comments, Charlotte began to look a bit teary. I think this was the first time that she had been given such an honor. Flora, Carla, and I began clapping and cheering and pretty soon everyone joined in. When we finally got to our good-bye song, we were a pretty emotional group.

My mom always says that it is important to give a person a second chance. I had never really agreed before. I thought back to that awful day in the cafeteria when Charlotte told me I didn't need to wear a brace. Then I fast-forward to this camp experience and realize that perhaps it was Charlotte who gave me a second chance. I had been so mean to her after that cafeteria incident, ignoring her hellos in the hall, avoiding sitting with her at all costs, and even giving her a few unkind looks. She turned out to be as supportive as Jean and Molly and then some, never once commenting if I made her late for dinner or anything else.

Mom and Dad arrived bright and early to pick me up. I asked them if they would mind hanging around until

Charlotte's parents came. Dad muttered something about not understanding women.

When Charlotte's parents arrived, my parents began talking to them as if we were related. Parents are like programmed monkeys; all they need is a signal. When it was finally time to say good-bye, I really wanted to hug Charlotte and tell her how much I appreciated all her help. Somehow, I think she knew.

As we pulled into the driveway, Mom reminded me that Conor was at an overnight with some of his high school friends and Mark had left for soccer camp the day before. I really hated the quiet, and Molly's house looked as if they had all moved out. Summer in Mayberry is not unlike summer in other country towns. Everybody kind of clears out. At least everybody I wanted to see was gone. Weirdest of all, I found myself missing Charlotte, who had gone from camp to her family's summer home on Nantucket.

CHAPTER FIFTEEN

Changes

August seemed to sneak up on me, and the first clue that it had arrived was the 95° temperatures, which sent my brothers and me to the family room in the basement. Our house is old and the only air conditioner is in my parents' bedroom. At least in the family room we could take out our sleeping bags and stay cool. Let me tell you, sleeping with two older brothers is no trip to the beach, if you'll excuse the pun. They did everything to convince me there was a ghost hiding in the laundry room. I almost believed them. Finally, Dad told them they'd have to sleep in the laundry room if they didn't stop.

Unfortunately, heat and my brace did not get along, and I ended up with this itchy heat rash. Finally, Mom gave Dr. Lebhar a call, and he suggested that I sleep in an air-conditioned room. Well, the air conditioner is Mom's most favorite thing in the whole word, not to mention how much my dad loves it. They eventually decided to keep theirs and buy one for me. I was so relieved. For a while there I thought I was going to have to sleep in their room in my sleeping bag. My dad is a snorer and even my mom complains about the sound effects. I sure didn't want to deal with that.

The air conditioner was fantastic. I could hardly get out of bed in the morning I was so comfortable, and my rash improved. Of course, I took a lot of heat from my brothers, the kind that comes when I have something that they wish they had. I was actually looking forward to getting back to school and being with my friends again. August seemed to be going much more slowly than July.

.⎯.

"Maisey, why don't we go school shopping tomorrow?" suggested Mom. "The stores are air-conditioned, and they are having lots of sales. It makes sense to do it now while there is a good selection."

As bored as I was, I really did not feel like trying on fall clothes in the heat. Besides, since I inherited my armor, I hadn't liked shopping. It's not as much fun since nothing seemed to look right on me, and I felt like Ms. Watermelon in just about everything I put on. That's an exaggeration, but really, it was just no fun anymore.

Finally, one day I agreed to go. The heat had lifted. Molly was due home in a week, and I was getting really desperate. Since I would soon be in middle school, I wanted to get a few dressy things: short skirts and blouses and maybe a dress. Well, let me tell you, it would have been easier to grow two heads. The styles were more fitted this year and finding skirts with elastic that had tops that looked OK with my armor was quite a challenge. Finally, I found two skirts and a very nice dress that was simple but just elegant enough for a dance or a special event.

Mom stayed outside the dressing room awaiting the final verdict. As I came toward her from the dressing room, I saw this very pleased look on her face. I went over to the mirror to get the full view and as I looked in the mirror I saw my mom's expression change as her eyes followed the length of the skirt. She kept staring at the hem. As my own eyes went down, I could see the problem. It was lower on one side than the other, lower enough for Mom to notice as well as me. I wanted to believe it was the skirt, but I could tell by the expression on my mom's face that it was more than that.

"What is it, Mom?" I whispered.

"I'm not sure, Maisey, but I think we should buy the skirt one size larger and then I can make the hem even all the way around. Put the dress on for me now so I can have a look at it."

The tone of her voice was gentle and yet I could tell she did not want to discuss the hem in the store.

The dress was longer than the skirt and so I didn't look so uneven in it. Mom commented on how great I looked in red and complimented me on my good taste. Out of the corner of my eye I could see her eye looking very carefully at the hem. Many times my dresses had needed hemming, but I never saw this look on her face before. I don't think I was imagining it.

As we moved on to the checkout, Mom appeared to be her jovial self, but there was something there that I couldn't explain. After we got into the car, this time it was Mom who was the quiet one and me who wanted to talk.

"Mom, why do you think the hem on my skirt was so uneven?" I asked.

"Well, Maisey, it could be your back and you know we are due to see Dr. Bones in September. Maybe we'll try to get in sooner. This is nothing to worry about. It will probably involve a brace adjustment."

As much as I wanted to believe my mom, all I could think of was the other "S" word, surgery. Oh how I wished Molly was around. The rest of the ride home I tried to think about what Molly would say, and then my mind wandered to Charlotte. As much as I wanted to call and see if she was home, I was afraid she would not understand my concern.

· — ·

The next morning I could hear this tapping and scratching on my bedroom door. All set to shoo away my brothers, I slowly began to open the door and was attacked by Molly, who started jumping up and down and hugging me.

"Molly, you came home early," I yelled.

As it turned out, I had gotten my dates mixed up and didn't realize that Molly was not staying at camp as late this summer. I forgot that her school had decided to open one week earlier.

"Go charter school," I thought to myself.

After we got all the camp news out of the way, especially the new turn of events with Charlotte, I told Molly about my uneven hemlines. She listened very carefully, and then asked if I had looked at my back in the mirror.

We carefully removed my brace and Molly held one mirror while I stood with my back facing my long dressing mirror located on the back of my bedroom door.

"I don't know, Maisey. It looks about the same to me. If it was really serious we could see it. I don't think you should worry until you talk to Dr. Bones. I think you need to just enjoy our last days of summer," said Molly.

She was right.

Molly and I talked so long that I forgot to eat breakfast. Mom made us a picnic lunch and we went out and feasted under the big elm in our yard. Molly still had a lot of embroidery floss left over from camp so we made bracelets all afternoon. Even my brothers left us alone. Conor had passed his life-saving course and was out looking for jobs for next summer, and Mark had already started soccer practice.

Molly and I spent almost every night together until finally, Mom announced that I had to go see Dr. Bones and she wanted me to get a good night's sleep. I was so busy with Molly that I forgot my mom had made an appointment. Part of me wanted to ask if Molly could join us, but I had a feeling it was better if just Mom and I went.

Since it was summer, Mom suggested that we go for a ride on the swan boats in the Boston Public Garden after my appointment. That was something we had done each spring with the boys for many years. While Conor and

Mark honked at all the ducks, I simply enjoyed watching the man who was paddling the boat. Although I was pretty big for the swan boats, I kind of wanted to see what it would be like without my brothers.

Our appointment seemed to go on forever. It was a scoliosis clinic day and all we could see were wall-to-wall kids with puffy chests. Finally, we finished up at X ray and were the next to be called.

As always, Dr. Bones was very pleasant, and he even commented on how healthy I looked with my nice suntan. He put the X rays up on the lightbox and stood there looking at them for a long time. As he studied them, he asked me if I noticed any changes. I started to tell him the hemline story and about halfway through Mom came to my rescue.

"Well, Maisey, it appears that perhaps your curve has increased a slight bit and so that's why there is a difference in your hemline. It's nothing to be upset about because we expect that these changes might occur even though we hope that they won't."

"What is Maisey's curve now?" my mom asked.

"Well, let's see, Mrs. MacGuire. I would say it is about 33° but there can always be a bit of a deviation."

"What's a bit?" my mom asked nervously.

"Could be slightly more, could be slightly less," responded Dr. Bones.

"Maisey, I'm going to have Tom add a slight modification to your brace, and then I'd like to see you back here in three months," he said.

"Dr. Bones, if Maisey's curve is worse, then what will you do?" asked my mom.

"Well, we have other braces, Mrs. MacGuire, such as the Milwaukee, or we may just continue with modifications. For now, let's sit tight and see how things grow."

The look on Mom's face said it all.

"Mrs. MacGuire, I know that you are concerned,' added Dr. Bones. "It is very possible that in three months Maisey will be the same as she is today. If for some reason that is not the case, we will talk then. For now, I would like to leave things as they are with just these few minor modifications."

We could both tell that Dr. Bones's meter was running since he had spent longer than usual with us. I was looking forward to seeing Tom, who appeared at the door just as Dr. Bones opened it.

"Hi, Maisey. How are you Mrs. MacGuire?" said Tom.

"I'm great, Tom," I responded.

"So, Maisey, how did you end up doing in softball?"

"Well, I did OK, Tom," I answered, very impressed that he had remembered.

"I told you that you can do almost anything with a brace," Tom chuckled. "Maisey, I need to take your brace for a few minutes so you and your mom can just wait here until I get back. It won't be long."

After a bit Tom returned and I could see a lump of padding inside the brace that had not been there before. He gently placed it on my body and explained that it would give me comfort.

"Watch for pressure sores, Maisey," he warned. "Don't wait until you are really sore to tell Dr. Bones."

Dr. Bones popped his head in one last time to inspect Tom's creation and then both he and Tom moved on while I finished getting my top on. Mom had gone out to make my next appointment.

As we drove out of the parking garage, the car clock said three. We hadn't even had lunch and somehow that seemed more important than a ride on the swan boats. Mom remembered a little place not far from the Public Garden. She even managed to find a parking space with a meter.

We had a quick, and I might add, quiet lunch, and headed for home. Mom was saying something about being ready for these minor bumps and suddenly, I was in another world. I was standing on the high diving board at our town pool making the most perfect dive ever and everyone was cheering.

I was awakened by Mark hollering in the car window, "Mom, can we go swimming?"

CHAPTER SIXTEEN

Middle School Adjustments

"Hi, Maisey, it's Charlotte. I was wondering which team you're on and who you got for homeroom."

I was so happy that Charlotte called. But before we got into the school stuff, I asked about her time on Nantucket after camp.

"Well, to be honest, Maisey, I was lonely after having such a wonderful time at camp. I couldn't wait to pack the car and get home," Charlotte replied.

"I know exactly what you mean, Charlotte. I think I am really ready for school and getting back with all my friends," I said.

We compared notes and discovered that I was assigned Ms. Semenetz for homeroom while Charlotte had Ms. Lynch, in the room right next to mine.

"Charlotte, what house are you in?" I asked.

"I'm in House III," answered Charlotte.

"House III? I can't believe it, Charlotte. I'm in House III also," I screamed over the phone. "Oh, Charlotte, I am so excited, So far, you are the only one of my friends who got the same house as me. Most of the others are in House II."

"I am so glad you called, Charlotte. I'll meet you in front of the side door first thing tomorrow morning. I'll be there by seven forty-five. See you then."

I really was glad that Charlotte had called. I was looking forward to seeing her in school. I had already filled in my other friends on my status with Charlotte so they wouldn't snub her. I told Jean how wonderful Charlotte had been to me at camp. I gently suggested that she be a bit more open-minded and flexible. She responded by telling me how much I sounded like a mother.

Molly popped in after dinner to see what I was going to wear the next day. She couldn't stay since her school had already started. When I told her about Charlotte being in the same house as me, she was very excited. I told her how Jean had reacted, and Molly started in on her psychology and told me that Jean was feeling "threatened." Sometimes it's kind of scary having a friend who thinks so deeply.

. ⌐ .

The next morning I couldn't believe how little I had slept. I didn't think I had fallen asleep until almost one in the morning, and then I kept tossing and turning. I was excited and nervous all at the same time.

Breakfast was without incident. Conor was still asleep since he didn't have to go to high school until the next day and the same was true for Mark at middle school. Only the fifth and sixth graders had to go.

While Mom packed my lunch, I ran upstairs and brushed my teeth. Then Mom came up and put my armor on. Although I truly wished I could at least go the first day without it, I knew better. Dr. Bones had made it very clear that I had to keep to my brace schedule at all times.

After the traditional first-day photos, I let Mom walk me as far as the other side of Molly's house and that was it. I went the rest of the way on my own. The middle school is in walking distance of our house, and I was excited about finally being able to walk to school. I was also pretty happy that I did not have to adjust to a new bus driver.

Charlotte and Jean were both waiting for me at the side door to school. Charlotte had a big smile on her face but Jean did not look quite so friendly. I was hoping that she hadn't given Charlotte a hard time. Jean rushed over to greet me, grabbing my arm and leading me into the building. Charlotte was trying to keep up but Jean wasn't making it easy.

"Hold on a minute, Jean. Let's wait for Charlotte," I urged, as Charlotte tried to fight her way through the busy hallway to keep up with us. As I attempted to say a few words to Charlotte, Jean continued talking.

"Oh, boy," I thought to myself. "I have a real challenge on my hands."

Jean's homeroom was on one side of mine and Charlotte's was on the other. For sure, I was the monkey in the middle. As we were saying our good-byes, Ms. Semenetz was standing at the door greeting her students.

"And who are you?" she asked, as I peered up at her short curly hair and warm smile.

"I'm Maisey MacGuire," I answered.

"Oh, Maisey. I've heard so many wonderful things about you. I am so happy to have you in my class."

Her comment really took me off guard, and I immediately thought of my brace. By the look on her face, I think she figured that out and quickly urged me to find a seat and meet the others.

I was rescued by Ivan, who hollered out, "Hey, Maisey. I brought my Twinkies and Gushers!"

Those of us who knew Ivan broke out into laughter. Fortunately for Ms. Semenetz, snack was not until later on in the morning.

The time went very quickly. Ms. Semenetz explained that we would have two teachers on our team, herself and a Mr. Anderson, who had been new the year before. Except for our "specials," like gym, art, and language, we would have either Ms. Semenetz or Mr. Anderson for all our main subjects. At the end of each day, we would have something called "team-time," when all the kids in House III gather and work on projects and other stuff. All in all, it sounded pretty neat.

We had to sit at our house tables during lunch, which I found a bit disappointing since I wanted to visit with my other friends. Charlotte could tell I was not pleased and suggested that I go around and visit with my friends at lunch recess. It was a good idea except I needed to go to the nurse and get my brace off then. Gym was right after lunch.

"Maisey, why don't I help you in the locker room?" suggested Charlotte. "Then you won't have to lose any of your lunch recess."

"Charlotte, that's brilliant. Are you sure you wouldn't mind?" I asked.

"Absolutely not. I promise," answered Charlotte.

Lunch recess worked out great. Charlotte was a little lost at first, but then Elizavoice and Fred started to talk to her. Jean had made a few new friends in her homeroom so she was letting go a bit. The morning had started out kind of tense.

After lunch the gym teacher, Ms. Gaderowski, met me at the door of the girls' locker room and asked if I had stopped by the nurse's office. I was so embarrassed.

"Charlotte was behind me and blurted out, "I'm going to be helping Maisey."

I was so relieved.

Ms. Gaderowski looked a bit confused, but then said, "OK, fine. I'll let the nurse know."

"Thank you so much, Charlotte. I kind of froze when Ms. Gaderowski asked me that," I said.

Inside the gym building were rows and row of stalls for changing, with curtains for privacy. Charlotte and I went to the very end of a row and as I slipped off my shorts, she got into her own gym clothes. Then she quickly and carefully removed my brace. I pulled up my gym shorts and threw a T-shirt on in record time. As we entered the gym, I was so happy to see that we were not even the last ones in. We both began to giggle, and I'm sure everyone else wondered what was so funny.

· — ·

Many things were different in middle school. The biggest change was that we no longer had to walk in lines down the hall with our classes. Everyone could walk as individuals or in small groups, and when the bell rang to change classes, we could even talk in the halls. Our special classes were called electives. All of those subjects were after lunch so our really hard work was in the morning. Then we had this teamtime thing, which I mentioned before. House III teamtime was at the end of the day. We got to work with all the House III students and teachers doing projects and getting help when we were having difficulty. Some of my friends would also be getting help from the resource teacher the way I used to.

My mom said if I had any trouble with reading that I could also have some help, but I was feeling I could do it myself. Sometimes I might need extra time on tests, but, hopefully, the teachers would let me have it the same way Ms. Staples had.

By the end of my first day I was really tired. It was about 90° outside. We were all roasting and dripping and looked like a bunch of overdressed marathoners by the end of the day. All the great hair looked pretty droopy, and once again I could feel my soggy undershirt sticking to my very wet skin. I would definitely need to bring some extra undershirts to school.

CHAPTER SEVENTEEN

A Field Trip and "Research"

"Middle school is so amazing, Molly. We even get to go on field trips in the fall instead of waiting until spring. Next week we're going to Faneuil Hall, Quincy Market, and George's Island. I'm so excited."

Molly and I always talk about school. We really talk about everything, but most especially school. Molly really loves it, and she often helps me out when I have a problem. For example, about two weeks into my new school year I was coming home dragging myself in the door with this book bag that felt like it weighed fifty pounds. Having a brace on your body and then adding a heavy book bag is no fun. Dr. Bones had made it clear to my mom that a book bag cannot cause scoliosis, but I could tell you that it sure doesn't make it comfortable. The bummer of it was that I really wanted to walk to school. Mark carried it for me a few times, but I think he felt kind of weird about that. I heard a few of his friends teasing him.

Finally, one day, I came home so wet and drippy and tired that I just wanted to cry. I went right up to my bedroom without even having a snack, and closed the door. I could feel the tears heading for my ears.

The phone kept ringing and I could hear my mom saying, "Maisey is taking a nap. Can she call you back?"

Finally, I dozed off to sleep. When I awoke, I heard Molly downstairs chatting with Mom. I still wasn't sure if I wanted company.

Then I could hear my mom say, "Molly, let me go up and check and see if she's awake now."

"Mom, I'm awake. Tell Molly to come up to my room," I yelled down.

"Maisey, I made cookies. Don't you want a snack?"

"I'll have some later, Mom. I'm not very hungry right now," I answered.

As I was finishing my sentence, Molly came into my room.

"Maisey, are you OK?" she asked.

Molly knows me so well that she can always tell when something is wrong. Her name could be "Radar."

"Molly, I am having such a hard time with my brace and my book bag. I feel like I have a double whammy with them."

Molly began to look both sad and serious at the same time. I could tell she was putting her thinking cap on. (Oh, no. Another of my mom's expressions.)

"Maisey, I'm going to run home and ask my mom what my sisters did. I was too young to remember."

Before I could say a word, Molly was off, and I could hear her skipping down our stairs. While she was gone, Mom came up and took off my brace. I quickly jumped in the shower, which felt so good on my sweaty body. When I came out, I saw the brace sitting on my end table in front of the air conditioner and Molly sitting in the chair next to it. She sure wasn't kidding when she said she would be right back. I had hardly gotten in my bedroom door when she began talking.

"Maisey, listen. My mom said that my sisters always had an extra set of their books at home so they never had to carry them with their brace. This is so easy. Just ask your teachers for another set of books."

"Molly. There is no way that I am going to ask each of my teachers for another book. I hardly know them, and it will be so embarrassing."

"No big deal, Maisey. Have your mom do it. She can go get them after school," Molly replied.

Molly was absolutely right. I could ask my mom to do it. Besides, she would be volunteering at school. She already knew some of the teachers.

"Molly, you're brilliant, as usual. I will ask my mom about it tonight. Thank you so much. If I could have a sister, Molly, I would ask for one just like you."

Thanks to Molly, within a week I had an extra set of books at home, and I was walking back and forth to school more comfortably. I'm not sure what my mom had said or done to get the books, but I sure was happy about it. I remember Dr. Bones telling me that this was a sensitive time in my life and that I would have ups and downs with the brace. I didn't mind so long as I had more ups than downs!

September went by so fast and I seemed to spend a good part of it trying to figure out if Ms. Semenetz and Mr. Anderson were an item. They looked like they were about the same age. Ms. Semenetz is tall and thin and has short brown curly hair and a very pretty face. She has these big brown eyes that look so warm when she looks at you. She speaks very softly and is strict, but in a very gentle way. She really knows her stuff.

Mr. Anderson is slightly shorter than Ms. Semenetz, but just a bit, and has a crew cut and heavy dark-rimmed glasses that are so ugly that he actually looks cute in them. He is always joking around, and you can tell that he really loves the science that he teaches us. He is also our math teacher. He has this expression, "Everybody get it or should I review it again?" We got into mimicking him in the hall saying, "Get it? Get it?"

We really think he is great, so we weren't doing it to be mean.

The real fun begins during teamtime when he and Ms. Semenetz are together in the same room with us. They sure seem to like working together. I know other students notice it, too. It is kind of fun when you realize there could be a romance going on right before your eyes. Once I even heard Mr. Anderson compliment Ms. Semenetz on her outfit.

"Go, Mr. Anderson," I thought to myself.

Middle school made elementary seem so boring.

. — .

Before I knew it we were on our first middle school field trip, off to George's Island and Faneuil Hall. Mom signed up as a chaperon. I was very glad about that since it meant that if the brace started to bother me, she would take it off and carry it in her tote bag..

The trip into Boston on the bus took almost an hour. It was a very warm, sunny October day, and the bus wasn't air-conditioned. When we finally got to Boston, the inside of the bus smelled so sweaty that we filed out in record time, giggling as we left.

We began walking from where the bus dropped us off to the dock, where we had to get the boat to George's Island. There were almost a hundred of us plus chaperons. What a noisy group. The boys were acting like something out of the *Goonies* and the girls kept checking in with each other to see who was going to stand next to whom on the boat. I was relieved that I only had to worry about Charlotte and a few new acquaintances that I had made since school began. Some of the girls were a lot more cliquey than my old friends from elementary school who were now in House II. Although Charlotte is neat, I missed Jean and Elizavoice.

We got onto the boat like a herd of elephants and Ivan was guilty of pushing the most.

I could hear some of the girls saying, "Who is he? He's cute but totally out of it."

Then someone else said, "Wait until you see him eat his Twinkies and Gushers!"

I started to laugh so hard that my eyes began to tear. Ivan looked over at me and even he began laughing. He is unique and I am glad that he is in my house. Ms. Staples used to tell him that even though he needed some better table manners, someday he might be the president of M.I.T. I agree. Ivan is so smart. He seems to know everything.

The ride to George's Island took about twenty minutes and you could smell the wonderful salt air and see the Boston skyline. I just love living near Boston, and it was so much fun to be here on a weekday. The tour guide who met us when our boat docked explained that George's Island dates back to before the Civil War. There is a fort on it called Fort Warren, which was used during the war as a prison. As we went into the chapel, we could see some murals, and the tour guide noted that in 1861 the song "John Brown's Body" was written here. My mother and a few of the other chaperons got all excited about that.

Charlotte and I eventually met up with Ivan, who was in the group that was behind us. Listening to Ivan reenact history as we hiked around the island was nothing short of hysterical. His chaperon did not seem to appreciate his one-man show as much as Charlotte and I did. Ivan is definitely going to do something famous someday. I am sure of it.

I finally got my mom's attention and began pointing to my watch. Everyone in our group was getting hungry and unless the Tall Ships decided to appear, George's Island was beginning to get very old. My mom was giving me her "Be patient, Maisey, look" but not for long.

This new boy, Edmund, who was also in our group, whined, "Can we go to Faneuil Hall now?"

My mom kept saying, "We'll be shipping out very soon."

I could tell that all Dad's talk about the Navy over the years had rubbed off on her.

We were sitting there waiting for the last group to arrive when I began thinking that maybe this was a good time to take off my brace. Faneuil Hall was going to be a quick walk around and lunch, and then the bus ride home. I knew I would have enough time to be out of it if Mom was willing to carry the armor.

I saw Mom talking to another chaperon, and I could tell she was in deep conversation. I knew Charlotte would be glad to help me. Finally, I caught my mom's eye and signaled that I needed the canvas bag. She quickly handed it to me as I grabbed Charlotte's arm, and we ran to the bathroom.

The bathrooms had this musty, damp smell and the floor looked like it had just rained inside. Charlotte hung the bag over her shoulder and carefully helped me out of the brace. Just as she slipped it in the bag, we could hear Mr. Anderson yell out, "Last call for the boat. We're leaving, gang."

My heart raced as I buttoned up the front of my top.

"Why hadn't I worn a pullover," I thought to myself.

Charlotte kept saying, "Hurry, Maisey, hurry."

Finally, I got it buttoned and we raced to the boat. Just as we were getting on, Charlotte looked over at me and began laughing. I had buttoned my top unevenly and it looked all crooked.

Before I could fix it, Ivan looked over to see why we were laughing so hard and yelled, "Maisey, dress yourself much?"

My mom came to the rescue, walked right in front of him and made a wall so I could fix it. Boy was I glad to have her around.

.⟶.

When the boat docked, we started to walk across to Faneuil Hall and Quincy Market. I just love Faneuil Hall. As Ms. Semenetz was pointing out that it was the "Cradle of Liberty," we were all breathing in the smell of pizza. The place they serve the food used to be stalls. Now it's a food market with all different eateries. While all the adults began to look up at the top of the building at the grasshopper weather vane, all of us kids began a low mumble as we began looking around at which place we wanted to go first: the shops or the food. Hungry as I was, I hoped to run up to Hog Wild, the pig gift shop, and check it out.

Finally, we got the go-ahead for lunch and "research," whatever that meant. Mom took a poll, and we all headed for Pizzeria Regina with about three other groups. The slices of pizza were huge and they tasted as good as they looked.

Charlotte was the only one in our group who did not have pizza. Although I was curious as to why, I decided not to go there. She had a veggie sandwich on this grainy bread and a yogurt, and she seemed pretty happy about it. I no longer looked at her diet the way I did before. You might say we had learned to respect our different ways. Never, ever has she made a comment about my junk food.

When we finished lunch, we only had about twenty minutes to run around and do our "research." As Charlotte and I were "researching" the store, we suddenly began to feel a tap on our shoulders. As we turned around to look, this masked pig face began snorting and grunting.

"Wait a minute, let me guess. Could this be 'Ivan the Terrible,'" yelled Charlotte. We all began to laugh and were eventually asked to leave the store.

As we began skipping down the stairs to meet the bus, with Ivan yards ahead of us, I whispered to Charlotte, "You know, Charlotte, I think Ivan kind of likes you."

Charlotte began turning red, and I was getting the idea that maybe the feeling was mutual. We quickly ran to our group just as Mr. Anderson was once again yelling, "Last call for the Mayberry group!"

Everyone was very tired on the bus ride home, and I sat there dozing for much of the ride. A group in the back began singing "Ninety-nine bottles of beer on the wall," which one of the mothers didn't like.

As we pulled into our school parking lot, I could see Mr. Briggs, our principal, coming toward the buses. I looked at my watch and realized it was just seconds before the two thirty-five bell would ring letting everyone know school had ended. Ms. Semenetz stood up and asked each of us to write a paper for homework on the importance of George's Island. It had to be at least one page, with three well-organized paragraphs. I was hoping that we wouldn't get homework, but this seemed to be a pretty manageable assignment. At least she didn't ask us to write on our "research" in Quincy Market.

Mom and I waited a few minutes in the parking lot for Mark, and then we headed home. I had been out of my brace almost four hours and I could tell that Mom was really watching the time. She is extremely organized about my brace and always holds me to exactly four hours.

From the very beginning she has said, "Maisey, we will all work together to help you with this."

As much as I wish I didn't have to wear the brace, I am lucky that my family is so together about it.

CHAPTER EIGHTEEN

You Win Some, You Lose Some

I decided to try out for basketball. Elizavoice said that all the girls would be trying out and that it would be a way for me to be with them again. I really don't get to see much of my elementary school friends since we are in different houses. I still get together with them some weekends, but I would love to be doing something with them in school.

Tryouts were going to be right before the Thanksgiving break, so that gave me a little less than a month. Conor and Mark were always shooting hoops out in our driveway, and I hoped they would give me some tips. My dad put in a net for them as a joint birthday present one year. Although I have played a little with them, I usually quit because one of them always gets bossy.

I thought I'd try to make a deal. I would make their beds on the weekends if they would agree to become my coaches. I ran this idea by Molly, and she thought it was a poor trade because there wasn't such a thing as "making" their beds. It's more like "remaking," since they sleep as if someone is chasing them. Even so, this was the best deal I could think of. The only other possibility was to eat their peas at dinner, but I hate peas just as much as they do!

Charlotte, who sometimes joins Molly and me for a weekend overnight, was very turned off by the whole matter.

"Maisey, why do you need to do basketball when you only have four hours out of the brace, anyway?"

"Charlotte, I know you would rather read a book, but I like sports and this is just one more sport I would like to try."

She seemed to get my drift.

While Conor and Mark gave me a workout, Molly and Charlotte sat on the grass cheering us on. They had gotten to know each other very well thanks to me, and we all had a really good time together.

In fact, once we went over to Molly's for dinner, and Charlotte started pointing out all the little jars of grainy stuff in Molly's kitchen and kept saying, "We have this, too. We have this, too."

Finally, I mumbled "good for you" and she gave it a rest. Then we all laughed.

School was going well, and I was really into the book we were reading in English called *Stepping on the Cracks*. It's about two girls who are friends and whose brothers are both soldiers in the war. Molly taught me never to share too much information about anything I am reading in case you also might like to read it, so that's just a nibble of what the book is about. I love it so much. I never dreamed that reading would someday get me so excited.

In social studies we were studying ancient Greece and I was amazed at the whole structure of their society. It was like entering a new world after studying the Native Americans and the colonists back in fifth grade. I was beginning to realize how big this world really is and how many different people make up the world. I wanted to learn everything about everyone, and I hoped someone was teaching them about me, too.

.⁐.

The days seemed to go by so quickly. Fall in New England is so beautiful, and my favorite thing is walking home from school on one of those beautiful October days when the sun is out and the fall breeze makes the orange and red leaves dance right out of the trees, sometimes in my path.

One morning I was sitting at breakfast and suddenly looked up at the calendar and realized that I would be seeing

Dr. Bones again. I was kind of bummed about going back to see him. What if things were worse and Dr. Bones said I couldn't play basketball? What if he made me wear the brace longer? What if he put me in the hospital for surgery?

I didn't have time to dwell on my worries since the teachers began to really load the homework on, and I was finding that I had almost no time for myself. Research projects were being handed out, and all I seemed to do was go to the library and do homework. They even had contracts with the parents to be sure the projects got done.

I had to have part one of my science project ready early because Mom and I had to go see Dr. Bones when it was due. I began to get a little worried about my visit. Yesterday morning I heard Mom say to Dad, "Bill, I hope Maisey's appointment with Dr. Bones goes well. Let's hope her curve is holding better than it did over the summer."

Normally, they don't speak about it when I'm around, but my mom thought I was still in the shower. I could tell by the look on her face when I appeared.

I was just back from the library, and I asked Mom to check over my spelling and see how my rough draft looked. We really could call Mom "proofer" because we are always asking her to help us.

When my dad asks if anyone needs any help, Mom always looks over at him and says, "Bill, you are letter-challenged."

My dad has problems with spelling and writes everything on the computer so he can use the spell-check. When I first found out about my own learning disability, he sat me down and told me how hard it had been for him until he realized that he was a very smart person. He told me about the teacher who really helped him the most, and it reminded me of my own third-grade teacher, Mrs. Lamonte. That year was a real turning point for me in school. It was the year that I really started to feel like a reader. For the first time I felt "smart," and Mrs. Lamonte was the reason. Nobody ever got me as excited about school as she did.

While I showered, Mom went over my paper. Then it was time for my brace to go back on. She reviewed my first draft with me and seemed pleased.

.－.

"Mr. Anderson, here's part one of my science project," I whispered.

He answered in a very loud voice, "Wow, Maisey, this looks great."

I was so embarrassed. Everyone looked over. He could tell by the expression on my face and lowered his voice.

"Sorry, Maisey. I get so excited about these projects. Good luck at the doctor's. There's no homework over the weekend."

The day went pretty quickly. Charlotte, who knew I was a little nervous, stayed pretty close. She had come a long way and made it a point to keep up with all the news about my back.

When I got home from school, Molly was sitting in the kitchen talking to Mom. Molly had a conference day and got out at noon. I was very jealous. Mom was busy making brownies, and I could tell that Molly had licked the bowl clean because she had this large chocolate circle around her mouth.

"Hi, Maisey. Your mom and I made you brownies and the batter is de-li-cious," yelled Molly. "The brownies will be out of the oven in ten minutes."

Molly gets so excited when she helps Mom cook.

Molly and I headed upstairs until the brownies were ready. She helped me get my brace off, which felt so good, and then we just relaxed in my room.

"Molly, I'm so glad you came over. I'm feeling a little nervous about my appointment tomorrow. Even though I don't want to have an operation, Molly, I really wish I didn't have to wear a brace. I can't buy any of the clothes that are in style because the brace won't work with anything but an elastic waist or something that is at least two sizes too big. I really hate it."

"Maisey, I think you have to put up with it all if it's going to help you," whispered Molly in her usual supportive manner. "My mother says that my sisters hated their braces even more than you because in those days they wore these big, clumsy things and everyone knew they had a brace on."

I'm sure Molly was right, but I didn't care about her sisters' braces. I only cared about my own, and I wasn't very happy with it. Being a kid is supposed to be fun and easy. I only have glimmers of that. When I finally learned how to deal with my learning disability, the letters on my paper ended up on my back. Now is that fair? I don't think so.

Molly and I chatted until Conor started pounding on my bedroom door.

"Molly, your mother is smokin'; you're late for dinner," yelled Conor.

Molly looked at me rolling her eyes, "He has such a way with words, Maisey."

The truth of the matter is that Molly's mother is never smokin' or angry at Molly.

"Conor, give it up," I replied.

"Maisey, Conor. That's enough," scolded Mom.

The trip into Boston the next morning was pretty easy. Traffic was light and Mom finally knew the way.

Once in the hospital we followed our normal routine. I ended up playing with a little girl who had braces on both legs. She was sitting on the rug trying to play with this maze thing they had in the play area. Normally, I didn't sit on the rug, but she kept looking over at me asking for my help. The time seemed to go by faster than I thought it would, and soon Mom and I were in one of the examination rooms waiting for Dr. Bones.

"And how's Maisey today?" asked Dr. Bones.

He is always so friendly, and I love the way he talks to *me*, since it is *my back* that has the problems. It always makes me feel important.

"I'm doing pretty well," I answered. He could tell that I was a little worried this time.

"Maisey, your X rays look much better this visit. Hopefully, the brace will continue to hold you."

"Dr. Bones, do you think this will continue?" asked my mom.

I already knew the answer was going to be one of those "wait and see" kinds, but I was anxious to hear Dr. Bones's response.

"Mrs. MacGuire, with a condition like scoliosis, we do a lot of waiting and watching. There is no crystal ball that we can look into and find our answers. Maisey has some growth left and ideally, I would like to think that the brace will hold her, and we can avoid surgery. However, the changes that occurred last summer are a clue that perhaps her scoliosis may be hard to hold with bracing. At some point we may have to look at something more aggressive, such as surgery. Bracing and surgery are our only options although there are those who might suggest otherwise."

Then Dr. Bones looked over at me.

"Maisey, you are doing a great job with all this. I know it is not fun to wear a brace, and I can only imagine how it is challenging your wardrobe. Keep your chin up and continue on as you have been. I don't want any dieting or anything like that. Go out there and have some fun. Any questions, Maisey?"

"Just one. Can I try out for the basketball team?" I asked.

"Absolutely. Go for it and shoot a few hoops for me. I'm a real basketball fan."

Then he looked at my mom.

"Mrs. MacGuire. I'd like to see Maisey in another three months. Please see the receptionist on your way out, and she'll give you a time. Enjoy your holidays."

Within ten minutes we were driving out of the hospital garage and on our way home. As usual, I dozed on the way while Mom listened to this weird book tape. I can't believe what parents call good literature.

I felt as if this incredible weight had been lifted after my appointment with Dr. Bones. I spent a good deal of the weekend perfecting my shots in preparation for the basketball tryouts. They were scheduled for the following week after school so I didn't have much time. Conor and Mark became my coaches, and I really appreciated their support. Even though they can be a pain sometimes, I really love having brothers, and I think they like having a sister. If for no other reason, it gives them someone to tease!

· ⁓ ·

"Maisey, rise and shine. You don't want to be late today. Remember, you have basketball tryouts this afternoon."

Mom was standing over my bed as I lay there hoping for just another ten minutes of sleep. I had had such a hard time getting there. I kept thinking about the basketball tryouts, and I just could not fall asleep.

Finally, I dragged myself out of the bed and within an hour was on my way up the street to school. I kind of wished Mom had offered to drive me, but the car was in the garage getting snow tires put on.

Charlotte met me at the front entrance to school and we walked to my locker. Jean came running over to me as I was going into homeroom.

"Maisey, are you ready for tryouts? They say only two sixth graders can make the team," she yelled.

The day went pretty fast. When the last bell rang, Charlotte agreed to take my brace off for me and stay until the tryouts were over. I appreciated and needed her support. While everyone else got into their gym clothes in record time, Charlotte and I escaped to the last stall. She took off my armor and gave me a hug for good luck.

As I walked into the gym, I saw my brother Mark sitting in the bleachers. I was pleased that he would want to be there for me. Fortunately, he had the good sense not to say a word. They seemed to be calling names in alphabetical order, which I was relieved about. I hated the time I had to be the very last one at softball tryouts. Finally, it was my turn.

"Maisey MacGuire," Ms. Gaderowski called.

All of a sudden I heard this "Wha, wha, wha" and out of the corner of my eye I could see Charlotte reprimanding Ivan. Just what I needed!

As the boys' coach started to throw balls my way, I began to tense up and I missed the first three baskets. Then I had to do a shot from center court and a foul shot. I missed the foul, but managed to get the center-court shot in, a three-pointer. I was thrilled inside, but very worried about all the shots I had missed. I hated that people could watch.

After the individual shots, they set up teams and let us play. I did better, but Jean was on a roll and kept hogging the ball. Jean is not always a team player and this was one of those times. I was relieved when it was finally over.

Mark waited for me and walked me home. As we were walking, he tried to make me feel better by telling me how great my center-court shot was. Unfortunately, the rest of my performance was marginal, and I knew it.

The Monday after Thanksgiving the team list came out. Jean was right up there as were a handful of other girls that I knew. Many of them were excellent players. Next to the names of those who made the team was a substitute list of some twelve girls. I was number eleven. I could feel the tears welling up in my eyes as I read my name.

When I turned around, Ivan was behind me.

"Hey, Maisey, you win some, you lose some. Cheer up. At least you made the subs list," and off he went.

I knew Ivan meant well, but I was far too upset to be happy about making the substitute list. Timing is everything in this world!

CHAPTER NINETEEN

Holidays, Flu-i-Days

I'm not sure how we got from Thanksgiving to Christmas so quickly, but suddenly we were baking cookies and making a Christmas list. Mom looked like a wild woman. It is my favorite time of the year, but also the craziest.

Charlotte and her family celebrate Chanukah, and I ended up being invited over to her house to share in some of the festivities. Her father sat me down and explained the whole history of the holiday, and I even got to eat potato pancakes, which they call "latkes." Charlotte and her family sang some very special songs and lit the candles on something they called a "menorah," a special candelabra with nine candles. It was so wonderful, and I felt honored to be included with Charlotte's family.

Charlotte had never been to any kind of Christmas cele- bration and so on the day that we decorated the tree, she joined in. She ended up spending the night, and she helped me and my brothers as we decorated the annual gingerbread house. Molly came over when we were almost done and added the finishing touches. Then, at the last minute, Mom let Molly and Charlotte spend the night.

· — ·

It was the last day of school before our holiday break. It had been snowing since early in the morning, and there were about four to six inches on the road. All the students were excited, but Ms. Semenetz was really stressing because she had to drive to Connecticut after school. I knew how far it was because my grandparents live there. I knew they wouldn't be up for the holidays because they were already in Florida, where all the old people seem to go. Granddad says that's not true, but when we went to visit them, everyone there was old.

Mr. Briggs went on the loudspeaker telling everyone about the rule against snowballs. It was like planting a seed. Why do adults always think they are helping, when in fact they are giving you an idea? The dismissal bell rang, and there was complete chaos. Snow always affects school that way.

Mark was waiting for me at the back door. The roads were slippery, and Mom had given him very strict orders about walking me home. I could really manage on my own, but I was happy to have him along.

· — ·

Christmas was right around the corner, and Molly was sick as a dog. I hadn't seen her in about four days. She had the flu. I stayed up too late myself because I woke up feeling kind of tired and achy, and Mark said that he had a rotten headache. When Mark gets sick, "rotten" is the word of the day.

Mom was looking a little stressed out and kept checking in with Mark and me on what she called our "symptoms." Mark really milked this. He had two pieces of cinnamon toast and two cups of hot chocolate in his bedroom. Normally, we are not allowed to eat upstairs. Mom offered me the same, but my stomach was feeling kind of weird. Meanwhile, Conor was running around singing "Jingle Bells" since he was sure that the stereo box in the attic was his Christmas gift. ·

By the end of the day, I was attached to a bucket, as was Mark. The very thought of food made me want to vomit even more. Conor was depressed being alone in his joy. How he loves Christmas. He kept telling Mark and me that he bought us each a great present. Present, schmesent. I could have cared less. I felt yucky.

Christmas Eve was a real bust. For as long as I can remember, we always go to the home of some good family friends. Conor really wanted to go, but Mom felt that Mark and I couldn't be left alone. Finally, Dad agreed to go with Conor and Mom stayed home to care for Mark and me. She really could have gone, because all we were doing was moaning and complaining in our beds.

It was finally Christmas morning and Conor came into my room at least five times before I could finally get my body downstairs to open presents. Mark was in even worse shape then me. Finally, we began, but I had to leave because I was beginning to feel dizzy.

Having a brace on your body when you have a stomach flu is the pits. Mom kept taking it off for a few hours and then putting it back on, but much more loosely than usual. After a few days she got hold of Dr. Bones, who told her she could have left it off for those first few days I was so sick.

"Oh, great," I thought. "Now she tells me this."

New Year's Eve morning arrived and Conor was also sick. Mark and I were almost up to opening the rest of our Christmas presents. Mom was also looking a little sickly and Dad announced that he wanted to go breathe some other air. We were a very pathetic group, for sure. It really didn't seem fair. In two days I would be back in school, which meant that my holidays had been "flu-i-days."

CHAPTER TWENTY

Bor... ing!

I'd been back in school for almost three weeks and I was so bored. Part of the problem was that I felt like I was living in an infirmary. Mom and Dad were sick as can be for almost two weeks after New Year's. Dinners were poor, and everyone in my house seemed so grouchy. I couldn't have anyone over because Mom said that maybe the guest would get sick. While Conor went off every weekend with the high school ski team and Mark played ice hockey, I just kind of hung out feeling very bored and annoyed. Even Molly refused to have me over for fear that her grandmother might get sick, which really bothered me since Molly was the one who had first given it to all of us. Well, not exactly, but she had spent a lot of time at my house that week that she got sick.

I talked to Charlotte a lot on the phone until Mark came down with the flu for the second time. I never, ever should have shared that with Charlotte because she started getting really weird and kept telling me about all these vitamins that my mom should have given Mark and all of us. When she started offering to lend us some of theirs, that was the final straw. I was so annoyed and surprised that Charlotte was "reverting back to past behaviors," as Molly would say.

In less than a week it would be February and I hadn't one exciting thing to share about January. I even looked forward to my schoolwork. Thank goodness Valentine's Day is in February, as is my birthday. That gave me something to think about. With my luck, there would be a blizzard and my birthday party would be canceled.

. — .

It was January 30 and it was snowing like gangbusters outside. School was canceled by nine o'clock the night before and if the snow continued, we wouldn't go the next day either. Mom said that if school were canceled, Molly could sleep over. I hoped her mom would let her. Her parents had just come back from a long trip and whenever they are home, they only let Molly over here for short visits.

Once I slipped and said to Mom, "Well, if they want to be with her so much, then why do they always go away and leave her with her grandmother?"

Mom gave me this terrible glare and told me I was "out of order."

"Great," I thought to myself. "My own mother thinks I'm a machine."

Even so, I felt bad for Molly. She seemed happy enough, but she spent more time with her grandmother than with her mother. That would be really hard for me, but Mom says that it is "unhealthy to judge others."

The snow came down harder and harder until finally, at eight o'clock, they announced that school was once again closed. I quickly called Molly to see if there was any chance she could sleep over. Her mother answered and said that they were just about to eat.

"Oh, darn," I thought. "I'm too late. They'll never let her come over after dinner."

Mom suggested that I have my dinner while waiting for Molly to call back. The boys were still out shoveling and would not be back for some time. Dad was sitting reading the paper and kept telling Mom how good the kitchen smelled. That's a hint that he's starving.

Dinner went by quickly. Mom had made a big pot of chicken soup with cornbread and salad. It was a perfect meal for a snowy evening.

It was my night to help clear the table. All three of us have these little jobs and for doing them we get a small allowance. The boys get more money because they have to do the lawn in the summer and the garbage every week.

Just as I was finishing up helping Mom, there was a knock on the door and Molly appeared with her tote bag in hand. Her parents said she could spend the night as long as she returned home by nine the next morning. I was so excited.

After a while we decided to go outside and build forts with Conor and Mark. That meant that there would probably be snowball fights, but we didn't care. Being outside at night when the snow is falling can be so neat. I just love it and so does Molly. She always walks around with her head back and her mouth open catching the snowflakes.

. — .

By the time I was back in school it was February and all the teachers were complaining that they were going to be way behind in their lessons. I was getting a bit nervous that they would decide to really pile the work on. Gosh, it wasn't our fault that it snowed. I was very excited that we would have February vacation soon and that it would be my twelfth birthday in no time.

There was still a lot of sickness in school. We had been assigned a big project in social studies, and we were working in groups of four. Charlotte and I were paired with Laquicia and Estrella. The four of us ate lunch together every day. Estrella was also a substitute on the basketball team, so she knew just how I felt when I didn't make the team. We were going to play in Tuesday's game.

Things at home had finally returned to normal. Well, almost. Conor just got his driver's permit and was learning how to drive. That is not normal! I couldn't imagine what it would be like to have the same brother that teased me all these years driving me. Mom said that it would be even weirder for her.

. — .

I began planning my birthday and decided to do a slumber party. I was allowed four friends. Mom and Dad were taking us out for pizza and then to a movie. I decided to invite Molly, Charlotte, Laquicia, and Estrella. At first I thought about Jean, Elizavoice, and Bug, but I almost never see Bug, and Jean and Elizavoice are practically attached at the hip. I really enjoyed getting to know Laquicia and Estrella, and of course, Molly and Charlotte were a given.

Molly's mom arrived, and I could hear her talking to my mom about my scoliosis. She was telling my mom all about Molly's sister, Darcey, who had surgery when she was four-teen. I was feeling very uncomfortable and somewhat worried since up until then I hadn't really heard Mom talk about surgery. I was beginning to wonder if she knew something that I didn't.

"Maisey, Maisey. Come on down and say hello to Mrs. Miller," called Mom.

"Oh, darn it," I thought to myself. "I really don't feel like this today. I like Molly's mom a lot, but something tells me this is a set-up."

"I'll be there in a minute," I yelled back.

Suddenly my mom was standing at my door looking into my room.

"Maisey, what is the problem. Please come down."

"Mom, I don't want to discuss my back with Mrs. Miller. I heard you talking about surgery a minute ago."

"Maisey, Mrs. Miller is here to see if you would like to go to Florida with them for a week in April. We just happened to talk about your back because Darcey will be here soon. What you didn't hear was Mrs. Miller talking about Meg, Molly's other sister, who didn't need surgery."

"Florida! Florida! Are you and Dad going to let me go?" I was so excited that I hardly heard her comment about Meg.

"Well, I think it certainly is a strong possibility. First I have to work a few things out, but your dad and I feel that it would be a nice treat for you."

I was so excited that I practically fell down the last few stairs as I rushed into the kitchen to see Mrs. Miller.

"Wow, Mrs. Miller. Thanks so much. I really hope I can go."

I could hardly speak I was so thrilled.

"Well, Maisey. Molly doesn't know yet. We are waiting to see if it's really going to happen and as soon as your parents say yes, we'll tell Molly. You know, Maisey, we leave Molly alone a lot with her grandmother, and we feel bad that she doesn't get to go away much with us. Her dad does lots of traveling for his job and I go along so I can see places. We're excited to be with Molly for a fun time, and we hope you can join us."

Before I could answer, Mom thanked Mrs. Miller and sent me off to finish "nothing." I got the distinct feeling that another one of those "mom" talks was about to happen.

As I lay on my bed I felt bad that I had judged the Millers earlier for leaving Molly with her grandmother so much. Now I saw them in a whole different light. I wasn't sure how I would keep this trip from Molly, but I would have to since I gave Mrs. Miller my word. Hopefully, Mom and Dad would say yes and we could start talking about it.

CHAPTER TWENTY-ONE

A Birthday to Remember

My birthday arrived, February 12, and I was so excited I could hardly focus on anything. The best gift of all had come when Mom and Dad said that I could go to Florida with the Millers. I couldn't believe it. Molly and I were out of our minds with excitement and we had already started planning what we wanted to bring with us.

Since my birthday fell on a Wednesday, my overnight party was set for Friday, which was also the beginning of our winter break. We planned a small family celebration, and I was hoping Molly would be allowed to come over. We have spent birthdays together since we were in preschool, which is when we first met. It's kind of neat having a friend that many years. Really, she is more like my sister, and the best part is that when we are tired of each other, she goes home.

Mom put a poster up in the kitchen of my little-girl pictures that said "Happy Birthday, Maisey," and on it was the day of the week and the time I was born. She does this every year, and I get more excited about the pictures than the presents. I chose turtle pancakes for breakfast, which pleased the boys. Mom is like an artist standing in front of that frying pan shaping each pancake. Dad came down singing "Happy Birthday" with this really silly grin on his face. Mark really teased him about it and told him he was in a league all his own. Dad just laughed.

Dad offered to drive me to school since he was running late and would be going right by it. I was happy for the ride. On the way he asked me the same question he always asks when we're alone.

"You doing OK with the brace, Maisey?"

And each time, just as I am about to really pour my heart out and complain a little, it's time for me to get out. This time was no different. Feeling a bit frustrated, I gave him this odd smile.

"I know, I know. We'll talk about it later, Maisey. Have a great birthday in school and remember you're my favorite daughter."

Obviously. I'm his only daughter!

I was feeling a bit sad about my birthday since Charlotte had been out sick and wasn't back at school yet and I didn't know Laquicia and Estrella well enough to know whether they would remember my actual birthday. Elizavoice and Jean might remember except I might not see them because of our busy schedules and going in different directions.

As I approached my locker, I saw all these balloons and streamers hanging out of it. Standing next to it was Elizavoice, Laquicia, Estrella, and Charlotte. I couldn't believe it.

"Charlotte, you're back," I screamed as the other girls sang "Happy Birthday."

Elizavoice handed me cards from Jean and Bug and gave me a video of the day I subbed on the basketball team. She had asked her mother to video it just for me. I just couldn't believe it. Ms. Semenetz and Mr. Anderson came out to see what the commotion was.

Then Mr. Anderson began to sing, but Ms. Semenetz quickly said, "Time for homeroom," and we all giggled.

My school day went by so fast that I could hardly remember what I did. All I knew was that it was the best, and soon I was waiting for Molly to arrive to join us for dinner and to open presents with me. Mom always gets a tiny something for the boys on my birthday, and I get something on theirs. It's kind of a neat way of including everyone. She had even gotten a little something for Molly.

My birthday dinner was delicious. I could hardly breathe when I finished. My present was a new bike, which we would pick up in the spring. I had always gotten my brothers' used bikes, and finally I would get one of my own. I remembered how dumb I looked on Mark's old dirt bike that had an orange dragon breathing fire on the frame. He had put bigger tires on it, and all I was missing was the leather jacket with the cut-off sleeves. I hated it. My brothers gave me a new helmet for my birthday since we are never allowed to ride without one. Molly gave me a pack for behind the seat, a great idea.

Molly's mother called for her around eight, which was a good thing since I had a lot of homework left to do. Conor and Mark also had work and thanked me for delaying it.

As I started up the stairs, Mom called to me. "Maisey, only one more hour left out of the brace."

Even on my birthday we had to keep to this annoying schedule.

. — .

Thursday and Friday came and went and soon it was time to pick up Molly, Charlotte, Laquicia, and Estrella for my party. We were going to the pizza place in the next town over, which has fabulous pizza.

"Maisey, Mom and Dad are waiting in the car for you," screamed Conor. "Hurry up or they'll cancel your party."

"All right, all right, I'm coming," I called down.

I couldn't figure out if the skirt I was wearing was hanging down more on one side than the other, and it was really troubling me.

"Oh well, I think I'll just wear slacks," I thought to myself.

I skipped down the stairs just as Mom was opening the back door to see where I was.

"Maisey, you were ready ten minutes ago. What happened?"

"Nothing, nothing, Mom. I just forgot to do a few things to get my room ready for my friends," I replied.

As always, the ride to the pizza parlor was an event as my dad talked to each one of my friends asking them strange questions. Finally, Mom gave him her elbow and he stopped. He definitely needs a script to talk to sixth-grade girls.

Mom and Dad let us sit alone at the pizza parlor, which I was so happy about. Dad only came by at the end to, of course, eat the leftovers.

Mom kept looking over and saying, "Bill, Bill, please."

We all started laughing. Dad, in his own businessman-like way, is quite funny.

The line at the movie theater was amazing, but since it was my birthday party, Mom had reserved the tickets. I quickly found five seats that were alone so that my parents would have to sit somewhere else. I wasn't trying to be mean, but get real. They wouldn't have wanted to sit with their parents either.

When we returned to our house, my friends and I were all ready for Mom's wonderful feathery fudge cake with that yummy maple-walnut icing. My brothers arrived as everyone was singing "Happy Birthday." Surprisingly, they were very appropriate, with the exception of Mark rolling his eyes a few times. They even stayed for the whole thing. Of course, they wanted a piece of cake. After cake we rolled out the sleeping bags, changed into our pajamas, and turned out all the lights so we could talk in the dark.

Molly and Charlotte checked out within an hour and so Laquicia, Estrella, and I continued to talk. Estrella was curious about my back and was asking me a lot of questions.

"Maisey, when did your back start to hurt? Is that why they put a brace on you or did they just say one day that you had to start wearing it? I mean how did you end up with it?"

I could tell that she knew nothing about scoliosis and that she had probably never known anyone with a back brace. Laquicia was very quiet as I retraced the steps back to the very beginning of how I ended up in this brace. When I explained about the fifth-grade screening, she blurted out, "Boy am I glad I did a good dive!"

I could tell that neither of them really understood. *I* understood because I was just beginning to get it myself.

Did it just sneak into my spine one night and say, "I've moved in and now things are going to be different 'back' there."

All of a sudden the room was very quiet and my eyelids were feeling like they had weights in them. The next thing I knew I was surrounded by empty sleeping bags and the smell of homemade waffles.

As I entered our kitchen, Mom looked over at me and teased, "Well, good morning sleeping beauty. Thought you'd never get up."

Laquicia and Charlotte were already dressed and Molly was upstairs getting her things together. I had forgotten she had to leave early. Estrella was still in her pajamas.

"How come you didn't wake me up?" I asked.

"We thought you might need more sleep now that you're a year older," teased Charlotte.

Everyone started to laugh. Charlotte was quite a comedy act and really came out of her shy self and enjoyed groups more. Even though she was kind of moldy about the flu and the vitamins, she is really a caring friend.

By lunchtime the house was quiet and everyone had gone home.

CHAPTER TWENTY-TWO

Good News

It was hard to believe that it was the end of March, and the snow was just beginning to disappear. Conor was thrilled because he had his driving permit, and this gave him a lot of chances to drive since the roads were not slippery. Mark had to stay home and babysit me while Mom took Conor driving.

School was very busy. We finished studying China and went on to ancient India, which I also found fascinating. We had a student in our class whose parents were born in India, and she shared lots of information with us. I loved that our school has all different cultures. It always makes it so interesting.

Once again it was time to go to Dr. Bones, and secretly I was very worried. The skirts we had fixed before school started did not look even. I knew that Mom had noticed, too, because I watched her as she stared at the hems in the mirror thinking that I wasn't looking. I was very anxious to hear what Dr. Bones had to say about this. It was all so weird because I didn't feel the change. It's as though someone is sneaking around rearranging the inside of your body. It really spooked me. We used to talk about inches in my house, and we would mark the door frame every six months with everyone's height. I·now found myself thinking degrees instead of inches.

· ‒ ·

The ride to the hospital was totally stressful. Dad went with us and drove, weaving in and out, which only challenged Mom's backseat-driver skills. By the time we got to the hospital garage, I wished that I had worn a blindfold and earplugs and most of all, that I had not eaten breakfast. I really felt like I was going to be sick.

Within minutes we were sent off to X ray, where we actually met up with Tom, my orthotist, as he was returning some images. I was so happy to see a friendly face and felt much better after Tom left.

Finally, my X rays were done, and we went to wait some more for Dr. Bones. I hoped it wasn't a long wait since Dad was very preoccupied, and even Mom looked a bit on edge. I wonder if it was because they were worried.

"Why did Dad come today, anyway? Something has to be up. I just know it," I thought.

When I saw Dr. Bones come out to get my X rays, I knew it was almost my turn. This time it seemed different. They didn't put us in an examining room for almost fifteen minutes. Finally, Dr. Bones came out. He had a corduroy forehead, and the look on his face was not so relaxed as in other visits.

"Hi, Maisey. And how are you doing today?" he asked as he looked over at my parents and shook hands with Dad.

"I'm doing OK," I answered.

"And how is the brace feeling these days? Have you been wearing it eighteen hours a day?"

His question made me uncomfortable and before I could answer, Mom put herself on autopilot and began this long speech about how on task I am about my brace and my time in and out. Oh, God, I was so embarrassed. I wanted to tell her to put a zipper on her lips.

Dr. Bones seemed to understand and quickly picked up that we were a very intense group this morning. Even I was feeling a bit that way. Then came the zinger.

After very carefully examining me and measuring my legs and watching me walk and bend over, Dr. Bones put my X rays up on the lightbox. Then he asked me to look.

"If you look up here at the X ray, Maisey's spine appears to be going through more changes and the degree of her curve shows a slight increase. It appears that her curve has increased by about 3°. Now please keep in mind that there is always a plus or minus 5° built into that.

Written up on the X ray was the number 36. That number was jumping out at me. Then I could tell that my dad, who is a real direct person, wanted some information.

"Now, Dr. Bones, tell me what could be happening with Maisey to make a curve that began at about 28°, then went to 33°, then stopped, and now is at 36° go through all these changes even with a brace on?"

Can you believe the length of my dad's question? It was like this long, long run-on sentence. Ms. Staples would have had a field day with it.

"Mr. MacGuire, I can appreciate your concern and there are many questions to be answered that lie within your big question. As I explained early on, 'idiopathic' means 'origin unknown.' There is ongoing research that suggests that this might well be familial. By definition, scoliosis is a lateral curvature of the spine, which can involve rotation. We really don't know why this happens. If we did, you and I might not be here today. What we do know is that bracing can, and in many cases, does minimize that process. In other cases, bracing is not as successful, and we ultimately move on to surgery. At the moment I suggest that we continue to monitor Maisey, hold her to her brace schedule, and hope for the best. She still has some time before she stops growing."

Dr. Bones continued, "Maisey, I know that is a concern for you as it is for all children who have this condition. Things are progressing along, and it is very possible that at some later date we may be considering surgery, but for now I think you need to relax and continue with your brace. In light of the way things are going, I will be decreasing your time out of the brace to one hour a day. Now, let's call Tom in and make a few adjustments."

While we waited for Tom, Dr. Bones chatted with my parents and me about day-to-day stuff and even though he is a doctor, underneath he is just like my dad, a normal kind of guy. I was glad that Tom got held up because it gave me some more time to get to know Dr. Bones. He even told me that he had a daughter and a son and some of the funny things that they do to keep his wife "hopping." I could tell that he really likes kids.

As always, Tom made our time together extra special, and I think he knew that I was a little worried. He started talking to me about my visit with Dr. Bones, and he began telling me about some of his other patients and how hard it can be to be in a brace. I really got the feeling that Tom understood my opinion about all of this. The whole thing just stinks. That's all there is to it. It stinks!

I could tell that Mom and Dad were feeling a little concerned because Dad stopped rushing to his meeting, and he even asked me if I wanted to go out to lunch.

"I want to go home and see if Molly is around if that's OK with you guys," I whispered from the back seat.

"Then let's do it," said Dad.

Mayberry here we come.

CHAPTER TWENTY-THREE

Fun in the Sun

The rest of March seemed to just drag. They were giving us unit tests in science and social studies at school, which were pretty yucky. And then, of all things, I got poison ivy. I think I got it traipsing through the woods one day with Molly. I had so much calamine lotion on that I looked like the "pink panther." It was even on my face.

Fortunately, March flew by, and Molly and I began planning for our week at Disneyworld. I was so excited about going away with her that I didn't think about anything else. I'm sure Charlotte, Laquicia, and Estrella were getting tired of hearing me talk about it. I caught them rolling their eyes at me a few times, and I felt bad.

We were leaving for Florida, and I was so excited that I could hardly stand it. I had a new bathing suit and sandals, tons of undershirts for my brace, a sundress that I absolutely refused to wear, and lots of shorts and tops. My grandparents even sent me twenty dollars for spending money, and I did little jobs for Mom to earn some more.

I felt kind of sad that Conor and Mark were not going to be able to see Disneyworld, but Mom said that she and Dad were going to take them to New York for part of spring break. At least they'd have something special to do. They were really excited for me, which was nice.

· ̄ ·

"Maisey, Maisey. Time to get up," whispered Mom. "The Millers are leaving in an hour, so don't fall back to sleep, dear."

I flew out of bed, and, after a lot of rushing around and many hugs and kisses from Mom and Dad, we were on our way.

Even though it was very early in the morning, the airport was jam-packed. There seemed to be people everywhere, and most of them looked very, very happy. You could tell they were going on vacation.

Finally, they were boarding us on the plane, and Molly and I sat about halfway back. Mr. and Mrs. Miller were across the aisle. Mr. Miller kept looking at me with this big smile and raising his eyebrows. What a funny guy.

Mrs. Miller was poking him saying, "Jack, leave the girls alone. They don't want an old goat like you around."

Molly started giggling really hard.

"Maisey, Mom has been calling him an old goat for years. It's her way, and he loves it."

After a while they came around with breakfast, which wasn't the most exciting meal I have ever looked at.

Mr. Miller looked over and said, "Maisey, you only have to eat it if you want it."

After nearly three hours the plane landed and everyone started to clap. It was exciting, and I could tell people were ready to "party."

Molly's dad put on this really funny straw hat and said, "Disneyworld, here we come."

We all started to laugh, including the people that were sitting near us.

The ride to the hotel was not very long. As we pulled in, I could see Disneyworld Park right in front of us. I couldn't believe it. We were staying right in Disneyworld. This was so awesome. I couldn't wait to tell Conor and Mark.

Our room was next to the Millers'. They called it an "adjoining" room. Mrs. Miller asked us not to lock the door between the two rooms for our own safety.

Mr. Miller laughed teasing, "Oh, lock us out. Have a party."

I was seeing a whole new side to Molly's parents, and I was really having fun with them. After we got settled, Mr. Miller took us down to the pool for a swim and suggested that while we swam and Mrs. Miller watched us, he would walk over to the park and get our passes.

. ⁓ .

The pool was amazing. It had this big waterfall that you could stand under and then a really long slide. Molly and I jumped right in. All of a sudden we looked up at the slide, and there was Mrs. Miller.

"Good-bye, everybody," she yelled as she slid down.

What a funny sight. Her beautifully done hairdo, which always looks perfect, made her look like she had a silver mop hanging over her face.

After a while Mr. Miller joined us and was just as much fun.

Then the alarm went off on his watch, and he looked over and said, "Girls, time for a brace break."

For sure, Mom had given them my schedule, and they were following it perfectly.

We got out, dried off, and Molly put my brace on. Then Mr. Miller suggested we go in and explore the park a bit. It was very warm, and I wondered how I would be able to handle the rides and stuff.

As we were walking into the park, Mrs. Miller looked over at me and said, "Maisey, I know from my own girls that braces make you feel pretty sticky in the heat. This park has some nice cool options we can go into and you should be able to have your brace off for dinner and the parade they have here tonight. We'll help you with the time. I don't want you to worry at all."

Molly's mom made me feel so at home and relieved. We spent most of the rest of the afternoon walking around and exploring. Molly's dad told me about this scary ride called Thunder Mountain.

"I love scary rides," I told him.

"Well then, Maisey, how about it?"

And so brace and all, in we went. Molly and her mom looked so surprised. I couldn't wait.

Mr. Miller and I liked Thunder Mountain so much that we decided we'd go back the next day. At one point my brace felt like it had slid up to my chin, but I think it was just the position we were in because of the speed of the ride. I was having the best time ever.

After the ride, Mr. Miller's watch alarm went off again, and he announced that we should head back and get me out of my brace for dinner. I couldn't believe how organized they were being about all this. Mrs. Miller seemed to read my mind.

"Maisey, we had a lot of practice with all this because of our daughters. Fortunately, your brace looks a lot more comfortable than the ones they used to wear."

When we got back to the hotel, Mr. Miller let me call Mom and Dad to let them know that I was safe and having fun.

Each day at Disneyworld was an event. Mr. and Mrs. Miller seemed to find something special for us to do each afternoon. Mr. Miller rented a car from the hotel, and one day we drove over to Sea World and on another to Busch Gardens, where Molly and I rode an elephant. Can you imagine? I rode an elephant. Its skin was like leather, and it felt more like my wallet than an animal. Mr. Miller took an awesome picture of us, and he said he would give me one when we got home.

Finally, it was our very last night, and I was so sad, but also getting kind of anxious to go home and see my family. I was starting to miss them, and I wanted to tell them about all our adventures. Mr. Miller arranged for us to go to a luau for dinner and a show later. Each of us would get a flower lei to put around our necks. I thought I might even break down and wear the sundress Mom bought me, even though I thought it has ugly colors. Molly said it would be perfect.

"All set, girls? Time to get ready for our last adventure," called Mrs. Miller.

When Molly and I walked into her parents' room I couldn't help but giggle. Each of her parents was dressed like they were going to be part of the show, and Molly's mom had done this weird thing with her hair. It looked more like we were going to a costume party than a luau. I quickly grabbed my camera.

The luau was something really special, and the Millers got right up there on the stage and danced. The whole audience broke into laughter and began clapping. Molly looked so proud and so happy. She has fantastic parents who really like being with her. They had done everything to make our week perfect.

· — ·

It was time to leave for an early plane to Boston, and I was making the very last Florida entry in my diary. Molly was sound asleep and had this funny grin pasted across her face. I hadn't slept because I was so excited about going home and telling my parents about my trip.

"Oh, Maisey, you're up already. You certainly are an early riser. Can you wake Molly for me? We have to be out of these rooms in about an hour, so we can get out to the airport in plenty of time," said Mrs. Miller.

After she left our room, I began trying to get sleepy head Molly out of her bed. Easier said than done. Finally, I got her up.

Leaving the hotel was hard. As excited as I was about going home, part of me wanted this week to last forever. I had not worried once about my back, and I had enjoyed Molly's parents more than I could ever say.

The airport was almost as crowded as it was in Boston. There seemed to be kids everywhere and a lot of them were really unhappy. The plane was even worse. It was wild. The flight was a bit bumpy because of something they called "low ceiling," and the kids on the plane were all pretty unhappy ... miserable was more like it. I couldn't wait to land.

Well, my airplane trip will always be a memorable one. We landed at Logan Airport in Boston, and they put us in a penalty box with two other planes because of some lightning problem that happened over where we were supposed to be. Everyone on the plane got real quiet when they told us, but then the kids began screaming and whining again. I like kids, but a pair of earplugs was looking really good to me.

Finally, we got out of the penalty box and "deplaned," which is a fancy word that means they let us out. My parents were out in the waiting area very happy to see us. After lots of hugs and funny stories we headed for Mayberry. It was going to be nice to be home again.

When we got home, I thanked Molly and her parents many, many times and so did my mom and dad. The Millers knew we meant it, and I'm sure they knew that I had had an amazing time. It was the most wonderful week I ever had.

Dinner went on forever. I really was ready to go to bed, but Conor and Mark wanted to hear every little detail. It was fun telling them. Then they told me all about their trip to New York, which also sounded great. We all just talked and talked.

CHAPTER TWENTY-FOUR

How Time Flies

I couldn't believe that it was already May and that I had been home from Florida for almost three weeks. I remembered Conor saying that the good thing about middle school is that the time goes by so fast. I didn't understand what he meant by that when he said it. The year had gone faster than any year ever had before. We were on our last book in English and about to go on a field trip to the Woburn Science Center, which has all sorts of animals. I couldn't wait since I love animals, all except for the skunk.

I made the softball team again, and I was playing well even if I say so myself. I had several really good hits. Dad said that I seemed to be "on a roll."

Charlotte and I had been talking about summer camp and about Laquicia and Estrella joining us. I might even have the chance to go for a month if my parents could afford it. They were going to let me know. I was definitely going for the same two weeks as last year.

Molly would also be returning to her camp which meant I wouldn't see her for eight weeks. I was feeling really sad about that because whenever I worry about my back and surgery, Molly cheers me up and gets my mind off of it.

I was also sad that, after this year, Mark wouldn't be in my school anymore. He was really good to me, and I think he kind of felt like he had to be the "older brother" because he never let anyone tease me about my brace. By the end of the year a lot of the kids had noticed it. I actually didn't care anymore, well maybe a little. I was getting used to it and having Charlotte around to help made it pretty easy.

The big news was that Ms. Semenetz and Mr. Anderson really were an item. My mother heard that they were engaged, but Ms. Semenetz didn't wear a ring or do anything to give us a clue.

May was winding down, and soon it would be Memorial Day. Molly was going with her parents to visit one of her sisters, who had just had a new baby. Can you imagine? Molly's twelve years old, and she's an aunt? Far out. She promised to bring back some pictures. Her grandmother would be going, too, so I would be picking up their newspapers each day. I was really getting lots of little jobs, but I wouldn't take money from the Millers after that great trip to Florida.

. — .

"Oh my gosh. I can't believe it. Are you sure? The ring is really on her finger? This is major, major news. I want to go and tell Jean and Elizavoice. Oh, you're right. Mr. Anderson might hear me. I'll do it later."

A major newsbreak: Ms. Semenetz and Mr. Anderson were engaged. How weird it was to know two teachers in the same school who were going to marry each other. You never really think of teachers as doing normal stuff like dating.

Lunch was really an event that day. Ms. Semenetz and Mr. Anderson could hardly get into the teachers' room to eat their meal. All the teachers were going up to them and I guess saying "congratulations." Ms. Semenetz looked like she was blushing. What a way to end a week, a month, and a school year.

When I got home I ran upstairs and called Molly to fill her in on the news. I was hoping that she had not left yet for her trip to her sister's.

I must have rung Molly's phone forever. Each time the answering machine came on, I kept hoping it was because someone was on the phone, but finally I gave up.

. — .

It was Memorial Day and Mark would be marching in the middle school band so we all had to get up bright and early.

Conor didn't even want to go to the parade but Mom said he had to. It's one of those family support things. Whatever. I didn't know what the big deal was because the parade only lasts about ten minutes. We're a small town so we're also a short parade!

After the parade we all went home and prepared for the annual family Memorial Day barbecue. It wasn't a really sunny day so I had a feeling we'd be eating on our screened-in porch, which suited me fine because there are always a lot of little bugs where we live. And let me tell you, they are hungry bugs. They sure get a meal out of me.

Even though the barbecue was good, the afternoon really dragged. Not one of my friends was home so I spent my whole weekend with adults. The boys were old enough to sort of go off on their own. I wasn't quite there yet. Well, I thought I was, but my parents disagreed.

At about six my phone rang. It was Charlotte. I was so excited to hear her voice. She had spent her whole weekend with her parents at their house on Nantucket washing screens and getting it ready for the summer renters. My weekend was really looking up after Charlotte's saga. It sounded like child labor to me!

Charlotte and I talked for almost an hour, and then it was time to get ready for school.

. — .

June in middle school is very different from June in elementary school. First of all, we had tests in almost everything the teachers could find to test us in. I was really having a hard time finishing all the tests on time and even though I could have more time, the other kids were always done way ahead of me. I didn't want them to think that I was that much slower. They might think I was stupid or something. Now that I had a brace, I was feeling even more sensitive about all this stuff.

The excitement over Ms. Semenetz and Mr. Anderson kind of died down. Molly was not as surprised as I thought she would be when I shared their big news. Anyway, I still thought it was big, big news. Nobody seemed to talk about their actual wedding but I was hoping I could see it.

Charlotte, Laquicia, Estrella, and I were doing a lot of planning for camp. Mom said that I probably would only be able to go for two weeks because of the cost. Once Conor got his license, they had to pay for something called insurance for him. Two weeks at camp would still be pretty exciting, and I thought Laquicia and Estrella would really love the place just as Charlotte and I did.

We only had a few days left of the school year, and boy was it ever hot outside. I was having a regular meltdown in my brace. One day I changed my shirt twice. Oh how I hated being twelve and having to wear an undershirt. I thought I might start calling them "brace" shirts. That sounded a lot better. What I really wished I could say was "bra" shirt. By sixth grade, girls are into bras not braces!

The last day of school I was to have all my friends, including Molly, for an overnight. Jean, Elizavoice, and even Bug were invited. I couldn't believe Mom and Dad were letting me have seven friends overnight. I would be going to the doctor a few days later, and I had a feeling they wanted me to leave upbeat. Whatever the reason, I couldn't wait.

. — .

My very last day as a sixth grader arrived, and I couldn't wait to become part of the upper house. I was a little sad though because it was Ivan's last day. He told us that he would be going to a private school next year. I had known him since kindergarten, and over the years having him in my class was like an adventure in eating.

For Charlotte, the news of Ivan leaving was really sad. I knew for a long time that in her own way, she had a crush on him, and I knew that Ivan liked her as a special friend too. They worked together on some of our teamtime projects, and their minds seemed to work in the same way. They both read these really hard, far-out science-fiction books and talked and talked about them. I just couldn't imagine what it would be like without Ivan at our school. Snack would certainly never be the same!

Suddenly the bell rang and I was no longer a sixth grader. Wow did the year fly by. I waited for Charlotte at the back door until I realized that Ivan was behind me probably waiting for her too. I decided to move on and met up with Jean and Estrella. We went as far as the corner of my street and then split up.

For sure, it had been a much quieter ending than fifth grade.

CHAPTER TWENTY-FIVE

Holding My Own

A few days after what was the best sleepover party I ever had, it was once again time to visit Dr. Bones. I had found myself distracted sometimes by my back since more and more I was beginning to realize that maybe mine was one of those spines that was going to keep moving. I had a feeling that my parents were thinking the same thing.

I noticed that my mom didn't talk much about my annual beach visit to my grandparents' house, and she kind of went day by day. She had gotten very picky about my brace time, even more than before. If I had on an open top, I would notice my parents looking at my back, and once my dad asked me to face forward with both my shoulders.

"What is he becoming, a drill sergeant?" I thought to myself.

Molly and Charlotte became the two people I could depend on when I was into worrying.

Charlotte really surprised me one day when she said, "Maisey, if you have to have surgery, you will do fine."

Was this the same Charlotte or a makeover? She had really come around and so had I. I even had my mom buy granola bars for her when she came over. Better yet, I even ate them with her!

. — .

Our trip to the hospital was now standard procedure. I knew my dad would also be coming, and I had a feeling that we would be a threesome until this problem with my back was finally fixed. Because it was summer, our drive was more relaxing, and I wasn't rushed out the door still eating my breakfast.

Strange as it may sound, I didn't mind going to see Dr. Bones and Tom. I saw them so much now that I kind of looked forward to the visits. Don't get me wrong. I got pretty nervous, but I liked Tom and Dr. Bones. I knew they really cared about me and only wanted to do things that would help.

Everything seemed crowded: the garage, the elevators, the check-in desk. Dad was telling Mom that everyone and their uncle might be going away to their summer places and wanted their kids checked out first. Mom was just kind of grunting back at his comment, and the two of them seemed like they were not paying attention.

We were waiting to see if I was supposed to go to X ray. There seemed to be some discussion behind the desk about my file. Dr. Bones was standing there talking to them. Then he was gone. The nurse was looking over at us and motioned to my mom or dad to come forward. My dad was at the desk in record time.

"Mr. MacGuire. You can take Maisey over to X ray. I am sorry about the confusion. The doctor will explain later. Here's the slip with the instructions for the technicians. If you get delayed, don't worry. We will be here until two o'clock."

While my dad was thanking her, Mom and I started toward X ray. I just couldn't believe how many people were there. There was only one seat left. Dad motioned to Mom to take it, and Mom and I kind of shared. Dad was standing against the doorway and of course, he was reading his paper.

There was a girl about my age who looked very excited to be there. She kept laughing and smiling and talking to her parents. They looked like they were having a party, not an X ray.

She looked back at her parents and said, "This could be it." Such weird behavior.

My turn was next. I was disappointed because I wanted to stay in the waiting room and see the other girl come out. I wanted to know why she thought having an X ray was so exciting.

After John, the X-ray technician, took my pictures, I waited for a few minutes to see if he needed to redo any. That was the routine. Then, if the pictures were OK, I got dressed. Finally, he handed me my very heavy pictures and we were on our way back to see Dr. Bones.

As we were being led into the examining room, that party girl was jumping up and down in the room across from mine and she was even hugging Dr. Bones. Her parents kept thanking him, and everyone was being so disgustingly happy.

When Dr. Bones came across to us, he looked at me and said, "Maisey, they are celebrating because after five years in a brace, she doesn't have to wear one anymore. Her spine has stabilized, and her Risser signs indicate that her growth has stopped."

"What are Risser signs?" asked my dad.

"Good question, Mr. MacGuire. Risser signs are indications of maturity. Our hope is that if we brace many of these children for a specific period of time and wait for them to mature, the bracing will be successful and surgery will not be necessary. As we have discussed before, for many children bracing is all they need, and they can eventually move out of the brace and never have another problem with their spine. As you know, however, there are exceptions. Bracing, however, has been an extremely successful method of treatment in many cases."

Dr. Bones took a quick look at my back and then went over and looked at my X rays, which he had posted on the lightbox, and then began measuring. Then he looked at my hips and my shoulders again and asked me to lie down on the examining table so he could check my back as well as my legs.

"Maisey, for the most part your curve seems to be holding this time. I know you are being excellent about your brace and wearing it faithfully. It seems to be doing its job."

I felt so relieved, and I could tell that my parents were in the same mode as me. They suddenly became very relaxed and friendly the way parents always get when good news comes their way. I kind of got a giggle out of it all.

We said our good-byes to Dr. Bones and moved on. While Mom set up the next appointment, I kept looking around the corner hoping to see Tom so I could share my good news. I didn't see him anywhere. I was a little disappointed but I knew that he had a lot of work to do for Dr. Bones and maybe for the other doctors.

. — .

The ride home was amazingly quick. There was no lunch offer because my dad had another big meeting at work. Instead, we talked about my summer plans and my annual trip to Connecticut to see my grandparents. My dad explained that my grandfather was not doing well and that instead of my going down for two weeks, the whole family would be making the pilgrimage. Inside I was so disappointed and sad to think that my grandfather was aging and that we wouldn't be able to do our walks to the beach. I was beginning to feel like I was getting a little old myself, if you know what I mean.

As we pulled into our driveway, my brothers came running out the door asking if I had to have surgery. I probably should have been annoyed, but it made me laugh. I know they really care about me and this was their own odd way of showing it.

"No, I don't have to have surgery. The brace is holding my back just fine."

"Go, Maisey. It's your birthday. Go, Maisey, it's your birthday," yelled Mark.

That's what he always says to me when something exciting happens. I have no clue where he got it, but he does it to Conor too.

Within minutes Molly was in my bedroom, and we were discussing our plans for the summer. We would be going down to Connecticut over the Fourth of July, and Molly would be long gone to camp. Charlotte's parents had decided to rent their Nantucket house for the month of July, so I was very happy that at least Charlotte would be around. Laquicia and Estrella were also going to be around.

"Maisey, that is the best news ever. I am so happy for you and so relieved that things are better with your back," said Molly.

"Molly, I'm a little nervous about getting too excited because I don't know what will happen when I go to see Dr. Bones again in September. Don't get me wrong. I am very, very excited, but a tiny part of me still worries. Do you know what I mean?"

Molly replied, "I do, Maisey, but I think you should just enjoy your good news and not worry. Remember, worrying is not going to help your back."

Another "Molly the mother" statement if ever I heard one. Molly was amazing and really should be one of those talk doctors because she knows just what to say. She could even do an afternoon talk show for kids called "Molly's Mumble." I really think it would work. Kids would be calling in every day and she could interview them about parents, homework, recess, what to eat.

I wanted Molly to stay for dinner but she was leaving for camp in only a few days and her parents wanted her home. Besides, I promised Charlotte I would call her as soon as I got home, and I knew she would be waiting to hear from me. More and more she wanted to know all about my back.

"Charlotte, it's Maisey. Great news. My back is holding, and my doctor never once mentioned the 'S' word. I am so relieved."

"Maisey, that's great. I guess the brace is really working out. I am so happy for you."

Charlotte sounded like she really meant it. I told her all about the girl who was so excited in X ray, and we both got a chuckle. Then we just talked about camp, which would be coming up in a few weeks. I told her about my grandfather and our trip to Connecticut. I knew she would understand because her grandparents were in their nineties.

. — .

Before I knew it, the Fourth of July was coming and we were packing the car for the trip to Westport to see my grandparents. Conor had just gotten his license and was really psyched about driving down to the beach so all the girls could see him driving. The beach is a five-minute walk so who drives there? Mom said that when I got my license I would understand.

The trip down to Connecticut took forever. Dad let Conor drive a little on the highway, and it was even worse than driving with my grandfather. Once, as my dad was nodding off, Conor picked up a little speed, and my mother began flipping out. After that, my dad kept his eyes open.

When we pulled into my grandparents' driveway, the house looked different. The gardens looked overgrown with weeds, and my grandmother didn't come out to greet us. My dad looked worried and instead of getting excited about being there, everyone was pretty quiet.

My grandmother met us at the back door and seemed very glad to see us. She looked tired and spoke quietly, telling us that my grandfather was lying down. I got the feeling that he didn't get up much. I had this very sad sense come over me, and I was afraid to go see what Granddaddy looked like. I think Conor and Mark were feeling the same.

Mom held my hand as we all went into the bedroom. Granddaddy looked like he had shrunk in the big bed. His scruffy beard was stubbles, and he no longer had the rosy cheeks that I remembered. It made me so sad, and for a minute I thought I was going to cry.

"Maisey, come over here and give your granddaddy a big kiss. I've been waiting for weeks for it."

As I leaned over, he gave me a big hug, and it felt so good to know that in many ways he really was his old self. Just a bit weaker. I took my shoes off and sat on his bed until it was time for lunch.

Lunch was yummy as always, but kind of sad, too. My grandmother shared how hard it was for her to care for Granddaddy by herself. She told my dad that the doctor wanted her to put Granddad in a nursing home. I could tell that my parents had already talked about that because Mom said that she had already found an opening in one near Mayberry.

"Mayberry," screamed Conor. "Then Grandma will be way down here all alone."

"Conor, Grandma is going to come and live with us after the summer. Then you'll be able to see her all the time, and Granddad will be close by in a nursing home. I am going to make the arrangements while we are down here," said Mom.

I had been so wrapped up in my back that I didn't know any of this. I guess my parents didn't want to upset us. I knew this meant that the Westport house would be sold and that our times at the beach might end. I was feeling very, very sad.

Conor, Mark, and I spent part of each day at the beach and some evenings. Mom and Dad packed up Grandma and Granddad and made arrangements for Granddad to be brought to the nursing home. He had to go there by ambulance since Dad was afraid something might happen if he came up in the car with us.

Saying good-bye to my friends at the beach was hard, especially to Shelley and her mom, and even Conor and Mark looked pretty down about it all. As we walked home from our last hide-and-seek game, Mark said how bad he felt for Granddaddy.

"I wonder how Granddaddy will do without Grandma there everyday?" he asked.

"Mark, I think he'll do OK or Dad would not put him there," I replied.

More and more Conor was sounding like an adult. I guess that might come with having a driver's license. I'm not really certain, but I think so. He sure wasn't like this before.

CHAPTER TWENTY-SIX

And Grandma Makes Six

Having my grandmother living with us was just great. Conor was happier than I have ever seen him because we had an extra car and he got to drive more. Grandma never liked to drive much and preferred to have someone drive her until she got used to Mayberry. She went to the nursing home every single day to see my granddad and stayed there until dinnertime. She really missed having him around.

Before I knew it my parents were driving me to camp. Charlotte, Estrella, Laquicia, and I talked on the phone almost every day discussing camp. I was so excited that I could hardly sleep. What a difference from last year.

Conor was working as a lifeguard at our town lake, and Mark had a job mowing lawns. He had three neighbors' lawns plus ours. They were both raking in the bucks! Conor even took some of his money and took this girl named Sharon out on a date to the movies. My brother dating! That was so weird. He even began getting haircuts without a scene from Dad.

"Maisey, are you all packed or do you need help," called my mom.

"I'm all set, Mom, so if Dad wants to pack the car tonight, he can."

The drive to camp was a breeze. My grandmother stayed with Conor and Mark so it was easy to get off. I really liked having her around but I felt sad about my granddad being in the nursing home.

It rained the whole way so traffic was light. It was definitely not going to be a beach day and so the bridge over to Sandwich was not backed up. Unfortunately, camp would be pretty soggy, which I knew from last year was no fun. Hopefully, Laquicia and Estrella would come prepared for the rain. I knew Charlotte would.

As we drove into the dirt road that led to my camp, I could feel the butterflies in my tummy. I was so excited. I waited all year for this, and I knew that Charlotte, Laquicia, and Estrella were probably feeling the same way.

"Dad, stop! There's Charlotte, and Estrella and Laquicia are getting out of the car next to her."

"Maisey, I can't just stop here. That girl over there is a counselor, and she is telling me where to park. You can see your friends in a minute," said Dad.

I already had my hand on the door handle, but Dad was right. The counselors had the whole drop-off thing down to a science.

"Charlotte. We have to park. Tell everyone to wait for me!" I yelled out the window.

We unloaded the car in a flash, and I was dragging one of my duffles behind me as I headed for my friends. Dad had already spotted Charlotte's dad, and they were all set to start talking when we headed them off by yelling, "To the cabins!"

Charlotte's dad really bonded with my parents and seemed to find everything in the world to talk about. Add Laquicia's parents to that, and you can imagine what it was like getting the adults to focus on the kids.

· ⌒ ·

Laquicia and Estrella were a lot more organized than I was that first time and seemed to settle in pretty quickly. The bunk situation had been worked out back in Mayberry so we were really all set and anxious for our parents to leave. First, we had to drag them in to get our stuff, and then we were ready to kick them out.

Just before they left, I asked Mom to go and tell the nurse that my brace situation was under control and that I had three helpers. This was so different from last year when I practically had a heart attack when Charlotte came screaming down the path. How we all laughed when I told Laquicia and Estrella the story. I even told Charlotte that I used to call her "Sugarless Charlotte," which really brought the house down (another Mom term).

After we said our good-byes and settled in, Mindy, our unit coordinator from last year, came by to say hello. Charlotte and I gave her a big hug, and she sat and talked with all of us for a while, telling Laquicia and Estrella all about the camp. Just as she was finishing, our new coordinator stopped by. They had a tendency to move them around, Mindy explained.

"Hi, girls. My name is Janet, and I will be in charge of you, ha, ha, ha, for the next few weeks. I have six brothers so you can imagine that I am pretty happy to be with a bunch of girls for a while."

I really liked her. Mindy left, and Janet sat with us repeating some of the stuff that Mindy had shared, but that was OK with me. Then it was time to go to lunch. Being in the same mess hall again was like going home. A lot of the cooks were there last year, so I felt like I was in a place with old friends.

Charlotte squeezed my arm while we were in line and said, "Doesn't it feel great to be back?"

"Yeah, it really does and I'm glad you're back with me, Charlotte."

Our first week was pretty damp. It rained for three days straight, and Laquicia and Estrella didn't look too thrilled. It had put a "damper" on a lot of the activities, including swimming, because there was thunder and lightning, too. If it rained again the next day, they would cancel our barbecue social with the boys' camp across the lake. That would really be a bummer. Estrella said they better not.

Finally, the rain stopped, and we all had a good, but damp, night's sleep. There seemed to be water dripping from trees everywhere, so trying to sleep became a drip, drip, drip rhythm. We were in the mess hall when it opened as was everyone else.

"People are rockin' and rollin'," yelled Estrella.

She was right. Everyone was joking and singing and they had these big smiles of relief all over their faces.

Charlotte got up for breakfast and yelled out, "This is a happenin' place."

We all laughed.

Molly sent me a letter everyday, which no one could believe. I was running out of things to write to her but Molly just kept on turning them out, and each letter was full of news. For a while my letters were full of rain talk.

· — ·

Our barbecue social with the boys was coming. There were mirrors in everybody's hands as we each tried to look as good as we possibly could. It was funny to look into each cabin and listen to all the conversations.

The trip over in the boats was a riot. All you could see were girls trying hard not to get wet or dirty. The counselors were feeling the same since they were pretty excited about seeing who was working across the lake. Last year I didn't even think about this, but this year I was much more aware. It was very funny to watch, and I was so worried about looking as nice as everyone else, even with my brace.

Charlotte thought the boys were better last year, but last year she looked like the very thought of a boy would make her vomit. I told her that, but she just laughed. Laquicia and Estrella knew one of the boys because he was a friend of their brothers. They seemed to be meeting a lot more boys than Charlotte and me.

"Charlotte, let's walk over to Laquicia and Estrella. I want to meet some of those boys," I said.

Charlotte and I made our way over to them and met so many boys that I couldn't even remember all their names. We played badminton and croquet and then listened to music. A few of the older campers even danced, but we didn't. It was a lot more fun than last year.

The ride home in the boat was so beautiful. The moon looked like a big, round, glowing ball of cotton, and it just lit up the whole lake. The lights from the boys' side seemed to sparkle. There were stars everywhere and before we got out of the boat we all made a wish. I wished that we could go to camp every summer for the rest of our lives.

The weather was great for the rest of my stay. Charlotte, Laquicia, Estrella, and I loved rooming together, and, when it was time to pack up and leave, we were all very sad. We had met new friends and done lots of things that we never did together before. Charlotte and Estrella even tried horse-back riding. I considered it, but wasn't sure I trusted a horse. Laquicia said she was afraid of heights and motion, and she was worried she might vomit on the horse, so she didn't go either. What a funny group we were!

. — .

Our parents must have missed us because they all picked us up at the earliest possible time. Even though I had had a great time, I was ready to go home. I was looking forward to being a couch potato for a while. My brothers were both working, and I needed to do my summer reading and go back-to-school shopping. Even though August seems like a whole month before school starts, it always whizzes by.

The ride home was like one big traffic jam, cars overheat-ing everywhere and lots of sirens and tow trucks. It was what my father called a "changeover" weekend and everyone was leaving the Cape at the same time. Finally, we got to Route 2, and I could not wait to pull into our driveway. I knew Mom would have some special homemade treat waiting for me.

"All out. Home sweet home," yelled Dad.

As Dad walked through the kitchen, he sarcastically com-mented, "Oh, I just love moving all your stuff myself. No, no. You don't have to help me."

"Dad, just leave it. I'll do it sometime later. I just want to have a quick snack," I replied.

Adjusting to being home again was pretty easy. I spent most of my time reading and watching movies, which I love to do in summer. The family room was cool, and the old couch was lumpy in a comfortable way. If the weather was good, we went to the pool and, if not, we just hung out.

A few times Laquicia and Estrella and I had overnights or went to the pool together. They knew Molly and Charlotte were away and were so nice to include me. Mom already knew their moms from my school, so sometimes, while we swam, our moms visited.

Each day seemed to go by faster than the one before, and soon it was time to think about being a seventh grader. I knew my house number this time because we stay in the same house for three years. My letter came announcing that my homeroom teacher would be Mr. Slais. Mark said he used to be a famous runner and basketball player. He's about 6 feet 5 inches tall. I'll look like a shrimp next to him.

Then it was time for back-to-school shopping. I wasn't really very excited since I already knew there would not be a lot to choose from. With this brace on for so much of the day, it's hard to get excited about clothes. I told Mom that I didn't want to make a day of it. Just a quick trip to the mall, some new jeans and shirts, and that's it.

Molly was due back any time now. Her school would be starting in less than a week. I was hoping Charlotte might be back soon, too. She said something about the end of August, since our school was starting earlier as well. I really missed them.

CHAPTER TWENTY-SEVEN

The Upper House

"Molly, I can't believe these teachers. I've been in school for three days and they are already telling us about a long-term project that we have to do on any country in the world. Do you know how big a report like that can be? And I have a whole chapter to read on Russia tonight. I am so stressed."

"Maisey, don't let them get you so upset. They know it's only the first week of school. I think they are just trying to give everyone a jump-start so that we know they mean business. The teachers in my school can be like that, too," said Molly.

I told Molly that I felt as if I had been shot out of a cannon.

"Maisey, in all the time we've been friends, I have never seen you so stressed about your school work. Just because you're in the upper house now, you shouldn't allow yourself to feel so pressured about school. You're going to do just fine. The teachers just want you to know that they feel you're getting older. It's a compliment, Maisey, come on. Can't you see that?"

Molly had her own unique way of looking at things.

"Molly, your mom is on the phone. She says you have to go home right now. You were supposed to be home earlier," called my mom.

Molly had to go. She had completely forgotten that she was supposed to come over for only fifteen minutes. She had "school rules."

After Molly left I took my shower and got ready for my brace. Mom came up to put it on. I told her what Molly had said about school, and we both agreed that Molly was a really positive person. She wasn't really a kid, and she wasn't an adult yet. She was kind of a "kidadul," a cross between the two!

Finally, I decided to go to bed and read my library book. I had enough reading to keep me busy for a year!

. — .

"Maisey, over here!" yelled Charlotte.

Charlotte was in the homeroom next to mine again and in two of my classes. I was very excited. Estrella was also in one of them. I couldn't believe it. As we walked to homeroom, I talked to Charlotte about all the reading they were piling on. She was feeling the same way, at least she said she was, which made me feel more normal about the whole thing.

"Just do what you can do, Maisey. Don't sweat it," said Charlotte.

"Charlotte, I can't believe you said that. You're a riot," I replied.

With that we went our separate ways and began our day. It was very hot out and my day was really dragging. I was in my second brace shirt, and my skin and the shirt felt like they were attached to each other.

"Could someone please tell me why they don't put air in these schools," I thought.

All our notes on reports would be graded this year, and, if you got a "C" or below, you had to stay after school and go to a class about taking notes. One of my teachers, Ms.

Lynch, was really getting into this. I'd be doing homework for hours.

When the bell finally rang, I couldn't wait to leave. Charlotte was close behind me, and even she was annoyed about the notes. In fact, everyone was complaining. Just as we turned the corner by the gym, I spotted Mr. Anderson.

"Hi, girls. How's it going?"

"Not so great, Mr. Anderson. We already feel overworked."

"Don't get discouraged," he said. "It's only the first week. Give it time."

"Did you and Ms. Semenetz get married yet?" giggled Charlotte.

"Go, Charlotte," I thought.

"Not yet, but it'll be pretty soon," he answered.

Charlotte and I were sure their wedding would have been during the summer. We kind of wondered when it was going to happen, but Mr. Anderson didn't say.

. — .

After I left Charlotte, I headed for home. I kind of missed having Mark in the same school. I always enjoyed talking with him about our teachers, especially the very first days of school. It was neat to compare notes. Mark had the hot line on everyone.

When I got home, Mom had baked a feathery fudge cake and so I knew, since no one had a birthday, something was up. My grandmother was at the nursing home with my dad. Granddad was not doing well, and Dad wanted all of us to go there before dinner.

I got this weird feeling inside me. I wanted to cry but I couldn't, and I felt like the butterflies in my stomach had gained weight. I had absolutely no energy, and I was feeling very nervous about seeing Granddaddy so sick.

Conor and Mark came in right behind me. I got the feeling that Conor already knew and that he had told Mark on the way home from the high school. Molly's grandmother came over with Molly to see how we were all doing. It must have been really scary for her grandmother, who was almost ninety herself.

We all went over to the nursing home around four o'clock. It was attached to a hospital, and they had moved Granddaddy from the nursing home area to the hospital. He looked bionic, with so many tubes attached. Our priest met us there, and we all held hands and said a prayer. Mark started sobbing, which got me going, and before long, we were all sobbing, even my dad. I couldn't imagine what it would be like if one of my parents died. I just couldn't imagine, but I knew kids in school that had faced it.

Mom drove us home at about seven o'clock while Dad and Grandma stayed at the hospital. We all kissed Granddaddy good-bye which was not easy because of all the tubes. His scruffy beard was the last thing I felt when I left. Oh, how I dearly loved him. I knew it would be the last time I would see him alive and so did Conor and Mark.

When we got home, Molly's grandmother had left us dinner. After we ate, Mom got out some old picture albums, and we looked at all the wonderful times that we had had with our grandparents. There were even some from last summer when I went down with my "armor," which is what Granddaddy had called my brace.

My grandfather was buried three days later in Westport in a place that is a stone's throw from where he was raised. Next to his grave is my great-grandparents' graves and eventually, my grandmother will also be buried there. My grandmother was amazing and did better than all of us, even my dad. She had plenty of hugs and kisses for all of us to get us through these days and was even joking about some of the things Granddaddy said to the nurses in the hospital.

"He was quite a character, your granddad," she'd say, and let out this funny laugh.

My teachers were really great about my grandfather's funeral and did not make me do all the work I had missed since some of it was review from last year. All in all, the upper house was pretty neat, and all the teachers told me how sorry they were that my grandfather had passed away. Even Mr. Briggs, the principal, stopped me in the hall to say he was sorry. I was amazed he even knew me, and he also said that he remembered my brothers. That was really something!

My friends in school were outstanding and all of them stopped by to meet my grandmother and visit with her. She loved all the attention and always had a batch of her wonderful cookies all ready. It was so weird. It felt like she had always lived with us. It was so normal, and all of us loved having the extra help when we needed it.

We went down to Connecticut almost every weekend after Granddad died. Grandma was selling the house and we all went down and helped go through the attic and pack all the rooms. I was the pots-and-pans packer. This would be the last weekend my brothers and I would go since we had too much school work and it was hard to pack up and leave on Friday and come back home on Sunday. As much as I loved it there in the summer, I liked being in my own house once school began. I think it's like that for most kids.

I decided not to try out for basketball again. I was really not that good, and I was pretty sure I would only be a sub along with almost a dozen others. Charlotte was doing performing arts, and I thought I might like to get involved in that too. They were doing a comedy and Charlotte said that it was fun. I couldn't believe she was trying out. That takes a lot of courage. I offered to do scenery since I absolutely love art. I wasn't as brave as Charlotte and to be honest, I might have had trouble remembering my lines.

My school days went very quickly, and before I knew it Indian summer had passed and fall was in full swing with a chill in the air each morning. Mom arranged for my extra set of books at the start of school, so my year as a braced student was going much better than the last year. Charlotte was a big help and was always willing to get me out of my armor at a moment's notice. Her interest in how braced life was going for me was quite something. I thought about starting to call her "Changing Charlotte" because she definitely had come 360° as far as my brace was concerned.

CHAPTER TWENTY-EIGHT

Thirty-Nine Degrees?

"Maisey, you'll need to take Tuesday off from school next week so that we can go see Dr. Bones. It's been almost four months since your last visit because we had to go to Connecticut. We absolutely have to keep this appointment."

I knew my mom was right. To be honest, after my granddad died, I began to see my brace in a whole new way. He was so proud of me putting up with my "armor." After I saw how sick he looked in the hospital, I decided not to complain so much. Even though he was gone, I knew it would make him really, really proud.

Tuesday morning we got up very early since the appointment was for eight thirty. I was amazed that anyone started their day that early. In order to get there on time, we had to leave Mayberry at seven fifteen. Grandma got up to see us off and to make sure the boys were not late for school. She let Conor take her car on the days she was not going to use it. Boy did he kiss up to her for that. It was quite something to see.

We sure did have the hospital routine down, and Dad even knew where to get the best cup of coffee as well as where to buy his newspaper. When you are the first appointment, X ray is a breeze. I was in and out in no time since I was the only one there. When we got over to Dr. Bones's area, he was waiting for us in the examining room. He scooped up my X rays and said he would be right back.

We ended up waiting almost ten minutes.

Dad kept asking Mom, "Pat, didn't he say he'd be right back?"

Mom just rolled her eyes at Dad which meant, "Cool your jets, Bill."

When Dr. Bones came in he had Tom with him. My dad quickly went over and shook hands with Tom. Then my mom told him how sorry we were to have missed him the last time. As Tom nodded, he moved over to me.

"Hi, Maisey. I got to see your X rays bright and early this morning. How are things going?

"Pretty good. I've decided not to play basketball anymore, Tom. I'm joining the performing arts group instead."

Tom said that he thought the team would miss me but that getting involved in performing arts sounded great. He said that he had done some of that himself in high school.

I didn't want to tell Tom that I had only played in one basketball game last year and that was why I was changing. Besides, I could tell that Dr. Bones's meter was running. You could hear all the activity out in the hall.

Dr. Bones examined my back while I was standing, having me walk back and forth to him. Then he had me get up on the examining table so he could look at the length of my legs and how they worked. Then he walked over to the X ray. If I read it correctly, the measurement said 39°. I could tell my parents had seen the number before me because they were waiting to jump in and ask Dr. Bones about it.

"Maisey, things seem to be progressing again. I know that you are being a champ about your brace, but sometimes the back has a mind of its own. I'm going to have Tom make a few modifications on your brace, and I want you to continue to wear it most of the day and night except for about an hour a day. I know on a melting hot day that might be a challenge, but there has been a break in the weather, and I think the warm days have passed," said Dr. Bones.

I sat there thinking about my last visit and how excited that girl had been about her X ray. Since my last visit had gone so well, I was hoping my back had done the same. Surprise!

Dr. Bones talked to my parents for about five minutes more while Tom went off to adjust my brace. I was so distracted by my curve that I only half-listened. I just sat there with this goofy smile pasted on my face thinking, "OK, folks, let's move on out of here!"

Tom stayed for a while after he adjusted my brace but suddenly there was a tap on the door.

"Tom, Dr. Bones needs you in Room 2."

Mom came back from making my next appointment and off we went. When we got home, Grandma had a huge plate of cookies waiting as well as some homemade chicken soup that smelled delicious. I told her about my appointment, and she told me about the time she went to the doctor and was told Dad was twins. Not exactly the same as scoliosis but I knew she meant well.

· — ·

Charlotte called after school to tell me about a book she was reading with the English class called *The Incident on Hock's Hill* about a little boy who only talks to animals. The boy eventually went and lived with a badger or something. It sounded pretty good.

The next morning I left for school a few minutes early so that I could get myself organized and back in the groove. Jean met me in the hallway, but I decided not to tell her about my appointment. She sometimes got dropped off early because both her parents work.

"Maisey, how come you're here so early?" asked Jean.

"No reason. Just having an early day," I replied.

I could tell that Jean wasn't buying this so I decided to catch up with my teachers later on. I visited with Jean which is something like reading the local newspaper. It is always amazing how much information Jean has about everyone and everything and how quickly she can spit it out.

When I caught sight of Charlotte coming down the hall, I felt so relieved. About halfway down the hall she saw me, too, and moved along a little faster. The first bell was about to ring which meant we had only five minutes to visit.

"Did you touch base with everyone, Maisey?"

"No, because I met Jean just as I was about to go into Ms. Grenthot's room. I sure didn't want her to be listening if Ms. Grenthot asked how my visit was."

"Maisey, it's not that big a deal. Just about everyone knows you anyway, and they don't care about your brace. You're getting too stressed about nothing," said Charlotte.

Charlotte was right. I really needed to chill out.

My day went pretty well after all except for my social studies teacher, who gave me reading that was due on Friday.

"Are we reading chapters or complete books here?" I thought to myself.

School passed, and the holidays were around the corner. I was glad I decided to join the performing arts program because I had a lot more homework, and I would not be able to do all those basketball practices. In English we were reading *To Kill a Mockingbird* which I found really hard. Mom read it with me in the evenings. I liked the story but the writing was so small. I thought I might never get through it. I was trying to get up enough courage to tell Ms. Grenthot, my English teacher, about my problem.

. — .

Over Thanksgiving Molly convinced me to tell Ms. Grenthot how difficult it was for me to read as quickly as the other students. I was feeling nervous but I hoped she would help me out. I went to school early to speak to her.

"Hi, Ms. Grenthot. Can I talk to you for a minute?"

"Good morning, Maisey. Well aren't you the early bird? How was your Thanksgiving?"

"It was great but I am three chapters behind in my reading. I am having a really hard time keeping up, and I am spending almost two hours a night on it," I said.

"Maisey, have you ever had trouble with reading before?" she asked.

"Well, yes. I have a learning disability called dyslexia and when I was in elementary school, I got help for a while, but then I didn't need it anymore."

"I see. Well you know there is another student in my class who is also having some difficulty and he is using the book along with a tape which our resource room has. He seems to be moving along quite well using both. Do you think you might like to try that?" asked Ms. Grenthot.

"Sure. That would be great. Thanks," I answered.

"Well then I'll arrange to get another tape, and I will give it to you in class today. Please be sure to return the tape when you are done, Maisey. It's very expensive."

School went pretty well after that, and I found that the tape and the book worked so much better.

. — .

I loved working with the performing arts group, and eventually Estrella also joined and did scenery with me. The performance was set for early January so we could work on it over the holidays.

Charlotte was a riot. We were putting on *You're a Good Man, Charlie Brown,* and Charlotte was Lucy. She walked around rehearsing her lines all day long. That was practically all she said to us. Even Jean was impressed with how much Charlotte could remember.

Soon our holiday vacation began. I celebrated Chanukah with Charlotte again, and Molly came too. Then they both came over to help us decorate our tree and the gingerbread house.

Christmas seemed a lot more normal than the last one when the flu bug got us. We all went to our neighbor's Christmas Eve celebration and everyone got up early on Christmas morning. My grandma said it was so exciting to be with us. I was sure she missed her friends, but I just loved having her with us.

Our house was chaos on Christmas Day because Conor and Mark got rollerblades and wore them in the family room the whole day. There was indoor/outdoor carpeting down there and they zipped around, bumping into each other and falling on the floor. I found it hard to believe they were in high school.

My favorite gift was a small compact disc player for my bedroom which I had seen back in August in one of the big discount stores. I was pretty sure I was getting it because no one asked me what I wanted for Christmas. Parents are so predictable.

The weather was a bust, no snow. Molly was at her sister's, and Charlotte went to Nantucket for New Year's. The lady down the street asked me to babysit for her troops and, until I heard what she was going to pay me, I wasn't very interested. When she told me how much, I agreed. I think if I had said no, Mark would have done it. I could see dollar signs in his eyes.

CHAPTER TWENTY-NINE

Nice Hips!

Even though January is my least favorite month, no one was happier for school to start than me. I knew I was not alone because everyone looked thrilled to be back. In English we were beginning *The Girl Who Owned a City,* which I am sure will be easier than *To Kill a Mockingbird.* I was going to try it without a tape. Mark said it was a great book so I was excited about reading it.

In social studies we were assigned another huge project, this time on the Middle East. Charlotte and Laquicia were in my class again but not Estrella, so we decided to have a group of three. We could still see Estrella in performing arts after school.

My brace had been feeling a little tight. Mom said I was what they call "premenstrual" and I was starting to develop a small chest, which I preferred to keep to myself. Even though we could loosen the brace straps, I didn't feel that it was sitting on my hips correctly. That could have been because I had gained a few pounds. My grandmother thought I looked very healthy. The school nurse agreed, but thought I had to see Dr. Bones since it was rubbing and I had a small pressure mark.

While Mom took care of setting up a visit with Dr. Bones and Tom, I was hard at work on my school projects and spent many afternoons painting scenery and getting ready for the big *Charlie Brown* production. I was sure that Charlotte was going to steal the show; she was so funny and so good as Lucy. Everyone was complimenting her. There were going to be three performances, Thursday, Friday, and Saturday night. Then there would be a cast party on Sunday, which would also be a work party because we had to take down the set. That means scenery in theatre talk!

Mom made the appointment with Dr. Bones. He could only squeeze us in in the afternoon. Dad was on a business trip so watching Mom maneuver in Boston rush-hour traffic would be a real show. It was a freezing cold day, and it felt like snow, but the weatherman said just cold air. Imagine Mom driving home from Boston during rush hour in snow?

Charlotte was so good about my back. She put my brace on and took it off very carefully so it didn't rub against the sore spot. She was almost better than Molly when it came to the brace, but look at all the practice I had given her! I knew I should be doing it myself, but it was always quicker with an extra pair of hands.

My school day went quickly, and I was off to my locker to get my coat so I could meet Mom. Hopefully, she would meet me right outside the upper-house office after she signed me out. I was not thrilled about that because so many of the kids hang around the house offices after lunch.

"Nice to see you, Jean. Tell your mom and dad I said hello," I heard Mom say.

"Tell Maisey I hope she gets good news," Jean replied.

I couldn't believe my ears. I could see the back of Jean coming out of the office, and I could only imagine what my mom had said to her about my back. Everyone would know that my brace was rubbing or worse, that I was having trouble with my back. Darn!

Mom met me at the door and could tell I was really upset.

"Hi, Maisey. You're all signed out, and I had a nice visit with Jean," said Mom.

"Mom, why did you tell her I am going to the doctor's?" I replied.

"Why, Maisey. I thought you had already told her because of the way our conversation went."

"Mom, you know Jean always does that. She was baiting you, and you gave her the fish."

Mom said there was nothing to worry about and that I was too sensitive. She thought Jean was very sincere.

I was very quiet on the ride to the hospital. Sometimes I wondered if parents were ever kids, because they just don't get it. I could tell Mom felt bad but I didn't want to talk.

Mom did very well getting us into the hospital in good time. Instead of sending us to X ray, Dr. Bones's receptionist told us to wait to be seen. We waited and waited and waited and, when the five o'clock news came on the television, I started to wonder if he had forgotten us. Mom, trying to be patient, got up a few times and spoke to the receptionist. Finally, it was my turn.

Dr. Bones apologized for the wait, and he looked like he had run a marathon. I told him where the brace hurt and he agreed as soon as he saw it that I had gained a few pounds and the brace was not fitting as well. He spent a lot of time looking at me in the brace from all angles. Then he took it off and took out his tape measure and asked me to lie down on the examining table. He carefully measured my legs and arms. Then he asked me if I had begun to menstruate yet. A bit embarrassed by the question, I shyly answered "no."

Then Dr. Bones said, "Maisey, I am going to have Tom re-form your brace a bit to make it more comfortable for you. I can see why you were feeling uncomfortable. I also want to talk to you and your mom about these latest changes.

"Mrs. MacGuire, when I first diagnosed Maisey, I mentioned to you some of the possible ways scoliosis may present itself. One of the things I discussed is called 'rotation,' which is when the vertebral column turns around its axis, which can cause something called a rib hump. The reason that Maisey's brace is rubbing is not because of her hips but because of a slight rotation that is changing the fit of the brace around Maisey's ribs."

"Well, Dr. Bones, tell me what all this means for Maisey," said my mom.

"Mrs. MacGuire, we have found bracing to be very successful, but there are those times when the spine does things that cannot be controlled by bracing. A curve like Maisey's has a two-in-three chance of progressing without a brace and only a one-in-three chance with a good brace program. This is very important for you to understand. It appears that Maisey is experiencing some increased rotation, which we may have to address surgically at some later time. For now, we will continue with her bracing program, which still seems to be holding her well. Rotation means she is *not* being held well.

There is one more thing I would like to mention to you, Mrs. MacGuire. Since surgery might be necessary at some later date, I'm going to ask you to consider having Maisey get an MRI to rule out any hidden causes for her scoliosis. The MRI procedure is very easy and takes about forty-five minutes. MRI is short for Magnetic Resonance Imaging. Maisey will lie on a table that moves partly into a tunnel. As the image is being taken, Maisey will hear a vibrating sound. There is no hurry, but it is something I would like you to consider."

Just as Dr. Bones was finishing, Tom arrived. He looked as tired as Dr. Bones, and he had this black apron on, which meant he must have come from his shop.

"Maisey, how are you doing?" said Tom. "I understand I need to do a little remodeling on your brace."

Normally, I love seeing Tom, but this time I was feeling kind of down, and I just didn't feel much like talking.

"Maisey, I know that you aren't very comfortable in the brace, but I think by the time I finish, you will feel much better," Tom continued.

Tom scooped up my brace and went off to his shop. Mom excused herself and followed Dr. Bones out of the examining room. I had this strange feeling that when she returned, I would be scheduled for an MRI.

I sat there in the examining room for quite a while feeling more tired than sad. It was way past six o'clock and Tom had just left with my brace. I was so hungry that my tummy was talking to me. Finally, I lay down on the examining table and closed my eyes.

"Maisey, make yourself at home."

I looked up, and Tom was standing there holding my brace. My mom was standing behind him with a big smile on her face. I was feeling a bit embarrassed.

While Tom put my brace on me, Dr. Bones stepped in and checked everything out and told Mom that he would see us in about six weeks. Mom told him that she had set up an MRI for early February and that we would be back to see him in early March.

The ride home was not as bad as we had imagined. Most of the heavy traffic had passed, and we moved along pretty quickly. Mom commented on how she hated driving in Boston in the dark because she still didn't know the roads that well. The real problem was that Mom had very poor map skills and would be the first to admit it. It had been a long afternoon, and she was feeling as tired as me.

The ride home got kind of tricky. It was snowing lightly and the road had just enough snow to make it slippery. We passed two accidents. I was relieved when we finally pulled into our driveway. I was also starving.

Molly had called three times and Charlotte twice according to my grandmother. I was so tired I just wanted to eat, shower, and go to bed. I didn't even care about homework. I was exhausted.

CHAPTER THIRTY

The Star

I only worried about my back for a few days, and then it was time for the dress rehearsals for *Charlie Brown*. Everyone was talking about it, and the scenery looked fantastic. Estrella and I had worked on it for what seemed like months, but we were very happy with how it all turned out. So was everyone else, which really made us feel good.

The dress rehearsals went very late. For the first time I could feel what it was like for the teachers to stay late at school. Most of my teachers made adjustments to our homework schedule because of the play, but a few did not, which made it kind of hard. The local pizza parlor donated pizza for our dinner each night, and in return they got a big advertising spot in our play brochure. Most nights I didn't get home until almost nine thirty, and then I would take off the brace, shower, get back into the brace, and go to bed. I think I was asleep before my body even hit the mattress.

Then I'd get up early and do my homework, and Dad would drive me to school. It was quite a schedule but it made me feel really connected to middle school, and I loved every minute.

Opening night came, and the butterflies in my stomach had climbed up to my throat. Everyone who had worked on the play had to go out on the stage at the end and sing a song. I was so nervous. Molly and her grandmother had promised to come early and sit right in the front. If I saw Molly, it would calm me down. My family would also be there sitting with them. In fact, my grandmother and Molly's grandmother had become very good friends.

Unlike me, Charlotte was calm as a cucumber (Oh, no. I'm picking up all Mom's little sayings). Charlotte was outstanding in the dress rehearsals, and she was the talk of the play. Nathaniel was playing Charlie Brown, and he was also excellent. He reminded me a lot of Ivan. The rest of the cast I never really knew very well until I got involved with the play, so I made many new friends. It was especially neat to know the eighth graders: when an eighth grader talked to you, you were considered "in."

The play was what my grandmother called "a smash" opening night. Nathaniel and Charlotte got standing ovations. I was amazed at how perfectly Charlotte had memorized her lines. Her parents were so proud. I was nervous when we had to go out and stand with the cast and sing the final song. Once I got into the first few verses I had a blast and, if the curtain hadn't come down, I would have stayed there. It was such an exciting night.

The rest of the performances also went well, but by the time the last one came I was absolutely exhausted. I found that carrying the brace around on my back sometimes made me more tired. I made sure Estrella took it off just before the final act so I didn't have to wear it out on the stage for the song. My mom came every night so she could go right after the play and scoop up the bag I put it in. We were getting pretty good at this.

Sunday's cast party was amazing. We played music really, really loud, danced, had all kinds of food, and ate the home-made desserts all the parents had donated. Then, when we were so stuffed we could hardly move, we had to take down the set and put everything back to normal. It was really sad when it was time to say good-bye. Our drama teacher, Joe Sprinkle, was the best and let us watch a video of the play while we were taking the set down. It was even good on tape. I was so pleased that I had decided to try drama. It had worked out so well for me, and I had gained many new friends.

Dad gave Charlotte a ride home after the cast party. It was hard for me to get a word in since he was like a news commentator interviewing her about her success as an actress. It was so funny. Finally, we pulled into her driveway.

"Charlotte, thank you so much for convincing me to do this. I have never been so excited about anything I've done in school. You are such a special friend," I said.

"Maisey, I loved having you as part of the play. Everything I do with you is always great. We are both lucky," Charlotte replied.

We gave each other a big hug and it was time to go home. I knew I would be dreaming of this for a long time.

CHAPTER THIRTY-ONE

The Inside Scoop

"Maisey, time to get up. We have to leave in about forty-five minutes and it is starting to snow," Mom was calling.

"Great," I thought to myself. "Maybe we should cancel."

I dreaded going for my MRI because I was worried about what they might find. My hems were not hanging exactly right, and I was also worried about my last visit with Dr. Bones. I hadn't really worried until the performances were over, and now it seemed like all I did was worry. I couldn't wait until all this back stuff was finished.

The MRI area was nowhere near Dr. Bones's office. In fact, it felt like we were down in a basement. It was quite a big area but there was almost no one waiting except us. We even had to ring a bell for the receptionist to come.

I had just changed into a johnny, and Mom was taking all her jewelry off and giving it to Dad. They said Mom or Dad could come in and sit with me. Since Dad loves to read his paper and have coffee, Mom would stay with me. At least I'd have her to talk to.

The MRI room looked just like an X ray room but with an MRI machine. There was this big cylinder, and a table that moved into it almost all the way. The room itself was cool so they would cover me with a blanket.

I liked the technician a lot. She gave us a tour of the room where the controls were and introduced us to the man in charge of them. She explained that she would talk to me through a microphone and that I needed to lie very still when the pictures were being taken and breathe normally.

Soon I was on the table and Mom was close by. We were about to begin. They had given me a three-minute warning that they were ready to start. The table had moved into the tunnel and I couldn't see Mom anymore but I could hear her talking. Far out! It sounded like there was a wood-pecker pecking under the table at about a hundred miles an hour. It was a good thing they had given me ear plugs. They were talking to me saying "ten minutes more," then "three minutes more," and finally, after a lot of minutes more, I was done. Altogether, it took about forty-five minutes.

After the MRI, I got dressed, and we headed for the hospital cafeteria for a takeout lunch. It was snowing hard and Dad was worried about the roads. Traffic would be backed up because of the weather.

On the way home I just sat and watched the snow which looked so beautiful over the Charles River, like a big white blanket. I am a real New Englander, and I just love snow.

"Maisey, are you asleep?" my mom called back.

"Nope. I'm just watching the snow."

"Maisey, I'm sorry that we had to come back in and do this today. Your back is very important, and we have to do whatever the doctors tell us to do. I know that it's hard when you have to take a day off from school. You may be able to make the last few hours but I am worried about the snow. It is really heavy," said Mom.

"It's OK, Mom. I think I'd like to go home," I replied. "Mom, how do you think I got this? Conor and Mark don't have it."

"Well, Maisey. I once had a slight curvature to my spine, according to Aunt Kate. I must have been very young because I don't remember, and Grandma never even told me about it. In fact, Aunt Kate told me in a letter she sent to me a few months ago after I had written and told her about you."

"What happened to your curve then? Did it just disappear?" I asked.

I kept hoping there was some magic way I could make mine go away.

"I suppose I still have it, Maisey, but it never got any worse. Remember what Dr. Bones said. If the curve is serious enough, it is braced, and if it isn't, the doctor just watches it. But I do want you to know, Maisey, that I wish it were me in the brace and not you. No parent likes to see anything happen to his/her children. Unfortunately, we don't have much say in it."

I felt bad for my mom. I knew how hard it must have been for both her and Dad. I guess being a parent could be really tricky sometimes.

The drive home was long and we all gave out a cheer when Dad got us home safely. He dropped off Mom and me and went to work. Mom didn't look too happy about that and he didn't dare stick his head in to hear what my grandmother had to say.

Molly came over after school and got a minute-by-minute description of my MRI. Her mom and dad had already explained it to her. They know a lot of medical stuff from Molly's sister and her husband. The only person more interested in my back stuff was Charlotte. Otherwise, I pretty much kept it to myself.

Between the MRI and the day we finally got to see Dr. Bones, I had a pretty exciting life. I turned thirteen and Mom gave me a little surprise party. The celebration wasn't like last year's but I like having something different each year. Mom again remembered to put up a poster of my little-girl pictures, which I love so much. School vacation was about to start, and I had so much work to finish before it began.

I don't know how I got it all done, but I did. Thank goodness for two snow days.

. — .

Our break was over and it was back to the old routine. Charlotte met me at the side door but we were hardly in the building when Jean came running up announcing that Mr. Anderson and Ms. Semenetz had married on Valentine's Day. Then they had gone off on a honeymoon. Unfortunately, our homeroom and classrooms were in the upper house so there was not much of a chance to spot the newlyweds. Charlotte and I decided we'd make them a card and stop by after school one day.

I could tell that school was back in full swing when I had a book report due, another social studies project, a new math packet, and a new book for English called *Handful of Time*. I felt like "a handful of time" was about all I had, too. On top of all this, I was due to go see Dr. Bones to hear about my MRI and to get my back checked. I was hardly excited about either. When they say that "March comes in like a lion," they're not kidding.

Molly was on overload too and feeling just about as out of time as me. Never had I heard her complain so much about school. Her parents placed her in a high-level program in January because they felt she wasn't being challenged enough in the other one. She had become "socially challenged" because she never had time to just come over and talk. Every time I saw her she had a book in her hand or was going home to read one. I felt kind of bad for her. Even my mom said she looked a bit stressed.

. — .

The next day was Dr. Bones and I was really nervous. Mom let Charlotte come over after school for a while. It really helped to have someone to talk to and Molly was so busy that there just wasn't time for us to talk anymore. But I had to admit that "Changing Charlotte" was really into my back and was as supportive as Molly and then some. She seemed to want to know every little detail and she never added any of her holistic comments. Mom said I was very lucky to have two great friends and she was right. In fact, Molly and Charlotte were more like sisters than friends. The only difference was that we never fought!

After dinner I put a movie on and just sat on the couch. I couldn't believe that my parents let me. Of course, it was short-lived because Mark really made a big deal of it and Mom finally gave in to him and told me to go up and read for a while.

"Thanks a lot, Mark," I commented as I ran up the stairs kind of annoyed.

Later on he came in my bedroom and said he was sorry but that he didn't know I had a doctor's appointment the next day. I don't know how he found out but I told him to forget it. I wasn't really that mad.

It took me so long to fall asleep. Those darn butterflies were back. Why didn't they flutter around in somebody else's insides? I tried to follow the route to the hospital in my mind and hoped that I could get lost on the way and fall asleep. It had worked before.

I must have driven to the hospital and back in my mind at least ten times before I finally fell asleep. I wasn't sure what road I was on when I finally went, but I was sure glad it worked.

"Maisey, Maisey. Hurry up. This is the third time I've been in here. We'll be late," Mom was saying rather sternly.

"OK, OK. I'm exhausted, Mom. Why do we always have to go so early?" I managed to respond.

"Maisey, please. Just hop out of bed and get yourself ready. Dad is all set to leave and so am I."

I got ready so fast that I couldn't even remember if I had brushed my teeth. Dad was driving as if we were being chased by the police and Mom was trying to slow him down a bit. The butterflies felt like they had moved from my stomach to my throat, and I was afraid if I opened my mouth to speak one would fly out.

I thought about closing my eyes and focusing on anything but the ride. This usually worked well and then no one would think they had to talk. I hate it when parents feel bad for you and so they think they have to talk. I preferred closing my eyes and experiencing the yucky feeling.

Dad made it in record time, which was no surprise. It was so early that the receptionist wasn't even in yet. Dad had this very worried look on his face. I sure hope he didn't start wandering around looking for Dr. Bones. How embarrassing that would be. Just as Dad looked like he was about to do something like that, I saw Dr. Bones coming around the corner.

"Maisey. Mr. and Mrs. MacGuire. Nice to see you. Thank you for coming in so early. I'm sorry, Maisey, if I cut short your night's sleep. I use this early slot so that I have a little more time to consult with families. You know the insurance industry has really put the pressure on medicine, which limits the time I can spend with families. If only they understood what families really go through and how important this time is to discuss and understand."

I had no clue what Dr. Bones was talking about, but my parents seemed to know and then my Dad was getting into it. He was going on and on about how hard it was not only on doctors but on patients and how children were sometimes being sent home from surgery far too early.

"Go, Dad," I thought to myself.

While they continued to talk, I was thinking about Dr. Bones not asking for an X ray. Maybe it was because they weren't open yet, but it seemed kind of strange.

"Maisey, how about we take off your brace and I take a peek at your back. You don't need a johnny. I can just gently lift your shirt if it's OK. I'll be careful."

I nodded and took off my top so he could see my brace and take it off.

"Maisey, your brace is fitting you nicely again since Tom made those modifications. Now let me take it off and see how the rest of you looks."

After Dr. Bones took off my brace, he asked me to face him. Then he looked at me from the side and the back. Gently he lifted my shirt to one side asking me to bend over. Then he asked me to walk in front of him and turn around and walk back. He began to explain what he was seeing, and I could hear the change in his voice.

"The good news is that the bracing has worked as well as can be expected under the circumstances, and I truly believe that it has challenged the progression of Maisey's curve to an even greater extent than we are seeing. What the brace has not been able to prevent successfully is the rotation that we are seeing, which seems to be increasing. Although we are very successful at fusions, we cannot surgically correct rotation. We can, however, stop the rotation by surgically fusing Maisey and putting in some instrumentation. This is what is done for those patients who have what we call 'decompensated' scoliosis. No matter how good the bracing, in this form of scoliosis, surgery is really our only alternative. At this point Maisey's curve seems to be at about 45° and I would say that it will increase about a degree a month."

Then Dr. Bones continued. "Maisey, I am recommending that you and your parents begin to give some serious thought to surgery. I know this is not what you wanted to hear, but it is a procedure that we have a great deal of experience with, and I have every reason to think it will be successful."

I stood there afraid to ask when this surgery might be and how long I would be in the hospital and out of school. I wasn't sure that I even wanted to know the answers.

My mom spoke next. "Dr. Bones, when are you thinking she should have this surgery?"

"Mrs. MacGuire. I think Maisey still has a little time. I am suggesting this be done not long after she begins menstruating, in the next few months if possible. The rotation is progressing but I think she can finish up her school year and maybe look toward summer. Please give me a call and let me know how you feel about this sometime in the next month, and then we'll proceed from there. In the meantime, if you would like to get a second opinion, please, by all means, do so."

The discussion between my parents and Dr. Bones continued for a while. I could tell that my parents had discussed this already. No one was asking me what I wanted to do. Instead, they were talking about dates, vacation schedules, number of days in the hospital, and more tests. I felt like I was going to cry, but I was trying hard not to. I sure wished Molly had come along. Finally, Dr. Bones could see that I was having a hard time with all this.

"Maisey, I have a feeling that this is not an easy time for you. How about if you go home and think about all this and speak to your mom and dad. Try not to worry because this is a surgery that we do all the time, and I feel confident that you will be pleased with the final results. In the meantime, keep wearing your brace."

· — ·

The ride home seemed to take forever. I could feel Dad looking back at me in his rear-view mirror and so I slouched down in my seat. I just wanted to go hide somewhere. None of this seemed fair.

I don't really recall what I did over the next week. I had lots of talks with Molly and even Charlotte about my surgery, but I could hardly remember what they said from one day to the next. Charlotte seemed the most interested, which surprised me, and she kept asking me so many details about my brace and what my curve was when I began to wear it. I guess she was trying to understand it all.

Mom and I had many talks about the surgery and how important it was not to ignore this problem. She even called Mr. Briggs, my principal, to see what could be arranged if I had to leave school a little early. I even heard her on the phone once arranging a visit with a new back doctor.

"Wait one minute," I thought to myself. "No one asked me about this."

A few days later Mom told me about the visit and said it was just for a second opinion and that I should not worry.

"Easy for her to say. I'm the one who has to undress and answer all those questions," I thought.

One day our school guidance counselor asked me to have lunch with her. I really didn't feel like it, but I figured what the heck. I decided not to share anything with her about my surgery, but when I got there I found out she already knew I might have an operation. At first I felt angry, but then we talked and talked, and she told me about other kids who had even bigger surgeries. One of the students had even given permission to give me her name. It was Bug. She had had a big heart operation in first grade, which I never knew, and she might need another.

March passed like one big blur. I managed OK in school, although I still kept worrying. Finally, it was time to go see the other doctor. He was also in Boston so it meant another big day in the big city. I hated missing school and most of all getting another back check. That's all I heard, back, back, back. Backed-up, back there, coming back, backpack, back brace. How I hated that word.

The second-opinion visit went quickly although I did have to have another X ray. The doctor was nice, and he also knew Dr. Bones and said I was in excellent hands.

"I'd go for the surgery, Mrs. MacGuire. Dr. Bones is moving in the same direction that I would move in and Maisey's Risser signs indicate that she is maturing. She should begin menstruating soon. Although we would ideally like to put the surgery off for a while, my sense is that considering surgery is appropriate, most especially in light of her rotation."

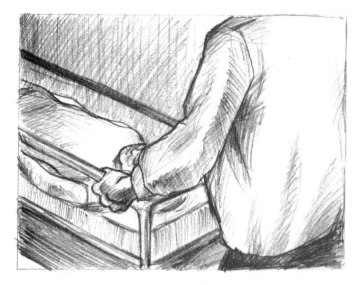

CHAPTER THIRTY-TWO

The Other Big "S"

My surgery date was set for mid-June. I had one more visit with Dr. Bones in May and then this thing they call pre-op would begin the day before my operation. Most of the time I just couldn't believe that someone was going to operate on both my back and my front. Two operations for the price of one!

I had a hard time concentrating in school, but my teachers and friends were great. I continued to meet with the school guidance counselor and enjoyed our little talks. In spite of all the worrying, I did well in school and the highlight of May was our overnight trip to New York City, which my dad chaperoned. It was amazing, and I could not believe how much we did in twenty-four hours. When we got home at about eleven o'clock at night, our parents looked like wilted plants.

I had to go into the hospital a few times to give my own blood before the surgery. Weird, huh! They keep the blood so that the day of your surgery you can give it back to yourself if you need it. Hospitals have some really strange ways of doing things it seems to me.

I went for my pre-op visit. Just as we were driving into the hospital garage, I began thinking about my very first visit and how Dr. Bones had that long, weird name I couldn't pronounce. It made me chuckle when I thought about what he told me I could call him. Some people at the hospital didn't even know who he was when I called him that.

The visit was a breeze. I already kind of knew how they would do my surgery, but I didn't mind hearing again. They wanted to do a few other little tests, and then we would go out for lunch and on the swan boats. Mom promised.

First we started with Dr. Bones, who wanted to have a few last words with us.

"Maisey, good to see you. How is everything going? I am happy that you have decided to go for the surgery. I really think you'll be happy with the results. You'll also be a few inches taller."

Dr. Bones spent some time going over how he would do the surgery and then more time talking with Mom. He kept looking over at me and giving me this big smile. I almost thought he was excited about finally fixing me, but I couldn't be sure.

Next we had to see this list of people who were checking me out to be sure that I was a healthy specimen and ready for the big "S." The first nurse I saw had this wonderful book and explained everything about my surgery and what would happen after. The pictures in the book were of real patients, so I felt she was telling me the truth. Then I was on my way to see the floor where I would be staying. They really covered everything. I felt popular, like a celebrity. Everyone was so happy to meet me.

Finally, we were done and were about to pull into our driveway. We would have gotten home sooner after the swan boats except Mom decided to try a new way home. Very bad decision. We got so lost, and the traffic just got heavier and heavier. Finally, Mom called Dad on her car phone and he got us home. What an ordeal that was.

"Look, Mom. There's a big sign on our door, and it looks like it has lots of names on it," I said when we pulled up to our house.

"Look at it, Maisey. It's wonderful. What a nice thing to do."

As we got closer, we could see all the names of my friends and teachers. I knew immediately it must have been Charlotte who did it. For the last weeks every time I spoke to anyone new she would ask me how well I knew them. Now I knew why. She was really an amazing friend.

Molly spent most of the evening with me and even Conor and Mark put aside some time to play a game of Monopoly with us. Of course, as always, Conor won. I didn't really mind. He always wins. At least this time he said he was sorry. That's progress.

When it was time for Molly to leave, I felt a little teary but she told me a joke and we both got into a giggle. Finally, my room was quiet, and I was just lying in my bed waiting for Mom and Dad to say good night. I knew if I didn't sleep well I had all the next day to catch up.

· — ·

Well, now you know my story, at least to this point. I always thought when the day arrived for my surgery I would be scared to death and a real mess. That isn't the case at all. Instead, there is a peace that has come over me because the thought of this being the last chapter of my scoliosis makes me very, very excited. Many kids have to wear their braces a lot longer than me; some have braces on different parts of their bodies for life. This has been a long haul and the thought of it coming to an end feels wonderful.

Now I certainly don't want you to think that I am not nervous. I have had those butterflies dive-bombing in my stomach since Dr. Bones told me that I was probably going to need surgery. He gave me a clue that it might happen and he told me that I might feel nervous or scared, but that each day I got closer to surgery I might begin to feel better about it. The best thing was when Mom called the National Scoliosis Foundation and got the name of someone my age who had had the very same procedure that I was about to have. I even got to talk to the girl on the phone. It really helped. She told me that she is now three inches taller than before and loves the way she looks. She said there was really only one bad day and the rest were OK.

"Maisey, can I come in?" whispers my mom. "We have to leave for the hospital in about thirty minutes."

How does she know I'm awake already. I hope she can't read my mind. She'll know all the stuff I've been lying here thinking about. Her radar can't be that good. Do you think?

"Is it OK if I open the door, Maisey?"

"Sure, come on in," I answer.

"Are you doing OK with all this?" Mom asks.

"I think so, but I really don't want to talk about it. That will make me more nervous. I just want to get ready and get going," I say.

"Sounds good to me," she answers.

One thing that really helps is that Mom gets a clue really fast. I know her next job is going to be to give my dad one. I dress quickly. Conor is now old enough to stay at home with Mark. No longer do they argue, because Mark wants to be sure that he always has a ride when he needs one.

The drive to Boston is almost too quick. It is so early that hardly anyone is on the road. Dad gets a parking space very easily in the hospital garage. It is really "choice" day and we can park almost anywhere. I'm not feeling very talkative, and I'm starting to get scared. I can feel my face getting red and hot, which is what happens when I am extremely nervous and scared. We walk toward the signs that say Inpatient Admitting. I am surprised to see so many people waiting in line to get in.

After a minute or two the nurse who had gone over my pre-op instructions with me comes over to me and says "Maisey, while your mom checks you in, why don't you come along with me, and you can get changed into a hospital johnny."

As she leads me into a small room and hands me a plastic bag for my clothes, she asks if I had anything to eat or drink since I went to bed last night. She seems pleased at my response, which is a big no, nothing.

As I come into the waiting area with this ugly baggy outfit on, another nurse asks all of us to line up to follow her to the surgical area. Dad quickly goes over and gets in line just as the nurse asked everyone.

"Please allow the patients to get in line first, unless you are joining them for surgery," she adds and laughs.

I'm not sure Dad realizes the hint was for him, but I am happy to see that he has dropped back quickly.

As I am getting on the elevator, I can see that the victims today came in all shapes, sizes, and ages; the smallest one is a cranky, whining two-year-old who seems very, very hungry. Within seconds I step out onto the sixth floor and into a big room that has beds lined up with curtains that go all around each one. A nurse greets us by our names and points out a space.

My space is at the very end and a nurse and a doctor are already waiting for me.

"Wow, they sure are in a rush," I think.

While we are all introducing ourselves, the nurse explains that she is in charge of my monitoring, and the doctor then adds that he is going to be the guy who puts me to sleep. He asks what flavor I want.

"I'd like bubble-gum flavor, please," I answer.

"Just think, you won't even have to chew," adds Dad.

Mom gives this nervous laugh as the doctor and nurse continue to talk to us. Then the doctor begins to put my lines in as he calls them. Then he attaches this other thing that has places to attach other lines. I'm trying to explain it all to you, but it's getting harder because I am beginning to get drowsy.

"Hi, Maisey, I bet you're beginning to get a little sleepy."

It's Dr. Bones.

"Now, Maisey, remember, first I am going to do an incision in your chest and then I am going to turn you over and make one in your back. I'm going to give you not one but two of my monograms. When we're all finished, you'll have some new equipment inside your body and a spine that looks a lot straigh . . ."

. — .

I'm not sure what his last word was because the next thing I remember is this room. I'm feeling very sleepy and there are nurses everywhere and all those machines. I can hardly keep my eyes open I'm so sleepy. Someone is asking me how I feel, and I can't even recognize who they are. My back feels kind of numb and my chest feels uncomfortable. I feel like I am going to cry.

"Maisey, Maisey. It's me, Dr. Bones. How are you doing?"

"O . . . K, I answer weakly."

"Maisey, your surgery was very successful. I think you're going to love how you look. I got a very nice correction and I think you've grown a few inches."

"Why is he talking to me? I just want to sleep, and I am so exhausted."

"Maisey, I know you're not feeling much like talking. In a few minutes the nurses will let Mom and Dad in to see you. They're very anxious to see how you're doing."

It seems like forever before I see Mom and Dad. It may have been only a few minutes, but I am so tired that I have completely lost my sense of time. I feel like I'm in one place and my body is in a whole different place.

"Maisey, it's Mom and Dad. How are you doing?"

I can feel someone holding my hand, and when I open my eyes I can feel the tears, like a flood.

"It's OK to cry. You've been through a lot and all the tears are probably tears of relief that this is all over," says Mom.

Mom is right. I had kept my feelings under wraps and hadn't really cried at all before the surgery. How I worried. At times in school I would look out the window and worry that something might go wrong. I never even told Molly about that. I was trying so hard to be a really big girl. It feels so good to finally let the tears flow. And boy are they ever!

I drift in and out of sleep for most of the night. If I wake up, I can see Mom at my side, sometimes half asleep herself.

I even remember Dr. Bones coming in a few more times. I don't think he ever sleeps.

"Good morning, Maisey. I'm Susan and I'm your nurse for just a little bit longer and then you'll be going upstairs to the floor."

I don't like the way I feel, and I think I want to cry all over again.

"Maisey, here's a button which will release medication to you any time you need it. We are also giving you something else to try to keep you comfortable. This will be your hardest day, and then I am told, it gets better and better," the nurse says.

Mom feels really bad, and I know she's upset that I had to go through all this. When Dr. Bones comes around the corner, she meets him before he even gets to me.

"She seems to be in so much discomfort. Is this normal?" Mom asks.

"Unfortunately, it is, but if she uses her button and keeps the pain medication coming, she will feel more comfortable. The first day after surgery is often the worst. We're going to move her up to the floor in about an hour. Once we remove some of these bells and whistles, we can transport her upstairs," says Dr. Bones. "We'll be leaving her chest tube in until tomorrow."

I like the fact that Dr. Bones is honest. He has been like this from the very beginning and so I didn't have any surprises. Even now he doesn't ignore my pain, but tells us this is normal.

· ― ·

The trip to the floor is uncomfortable, and no one is happier than me to be in one place for a while. Any little bump is a reminder that my back is very tender. My room is across from the nurses' station, so it is a bit noisy, but I enjoy the distraction of the activity. My roommate is a girl named Shakayla, who had the exact same surgery as me, but two days ago. She's about two years older than me and has the same taste in music.

"Maisey, today is going to be a tough day for you so I'm not going to talk to you a lot. Tomorrow will be a lot better, especially once you get up and go to the bathroom on your own," says Shakayla.

The bathroom. Oh my gosh. I hadn't even thought of the bathroom. I'd rather wet the bed than get up and walk to the bathroom. Shakayla seems to be reading my mind.

"Maisey, I promise you by tomorrow what seems impossible today will be fine."

I want to believe her, but I'm just not convinced this can be true.

My brothers and my dad arrive after lunch. Conor tells me that Molly also wants to come, but her mom said it's too soon. That really annoys me but after about fifteen minutes of company, I can't wait for the boys and Dad to leave. Mom is going to stay the night and so is Shakayla's mom. They have these special fold-out beds in another room for the parents. Sometimes, you can even stay in the room, but the hospital is too full.

I have spent most of today sleeping. Shakayla has had a lot of company, but they have been very quiet and when they get noisy, I can hear Shakayla's mom telling them that I am only a day out of surgery. I can't wait until I feel and look as good as Shakayla, especially since her surgery was two hours longer than mine.

At times the pain medication does not seem to work fast enough. They came in and gave me a shot that they said would relax my muscles. I have never been so happy about a needle in my whole life. It really is helping a lot.

I eat my whole dinner, which really surprises me. It's chicken soup, grilled cheese, jello, and peaches. They keep asking me to blow into this thing that has plastic balls in it to keep my lungs clear. I must admit that when I do it after a meal, it makes me nauseous.

Shakayla looks over and says, "Maisey, that's not something you do right after eating."

"No kidding," I think to myself.

After dinner I feel better. I am not excited about the bedpan, but Shakayla promises me that after tonight, I'll be back on a toilet. She has a great sense of humor and I enjoy hearing about her back. She wore her brace for almost four years. Each time they thought they'd operate, it looked better. Then, finally, it just got worse and worse. She says that one day she looked in the mirror at her clunky brace and said, "I feel so ugly in this. I want that surgery."

Eventually, the degree of her curve progressed so much that the surgery had to be done. Dr. Bones operated on her, too.

While Shakayla and I talk, Mom and Shakayla's mom, Deborah, chat. Oh boy do they chat. They cover everything from cooking to men. Every once in a while Shakayla and I listen and just laugh until our backs hurt too much.

· ‒ ·

This morning they are getting me out of bed. The nurse says I will be able to go home in a few days.

"Get serious," I think to myself. "Three days and I haven't even gone to the bathroom on my own."

Believe me, these nurses have a line to your brain because I am now on my way to the bathroom. I am so uncomfortable and my legs feel like rubber. Mom is in the background mumbling "I hope it's not too soon for her to be out of bed."

Being able to get up and move around feels so wonderful. The nurse washed me and helped me get organized so I can brush my teeth from the sink. Now I am actually sitting in a chair and Charlotte is due to arrive any minute with Molly. Get this. It's Charlotte's mom and dad who are driving them in. Isn't that something?

Seeing Charlotte and Molly is wonderful and they are so happy to meet Shakayla, who has entertained us every minute. She makes everything seem so funny.

Something weird seems to be going on outside the room, though. Charlotte's mom and dad have been talking to my mom outside my room for almost an hour now. They look so serious. What is going on?

Charlotte and Molly stay for almost two hours. Just as they are leaving, Dad and my brothers arrive. While Conor and Mark visit with me and Shakayla, Mom is outside talking very seriously with Dad.

Dr. Bones comes in to check on Shakayla and me just before my parents and my brothers leave to get dinner for themselves. He tells both of us that we are "model patients." He has a few other people with him who just follow behind and hardly speak. As they trail behind him out our door, Shakayla looks over at me and says, "rookies. They're the rookies. You know, trainees."

Then we both laugh.

Today I am feeling much better, and they have taken the bandages off my back and my front. Now I have a very small one on each side. I still use my pain button a little, and I can't imagine not having it. Dr. Bones came in early this morning and gave Shakayla her "walking papers." She can go home now. I am sad about that. She lives much closer to Boston than me and we may never see each other again. I'm giving her my dad's e-mail address, and she has given me hers. Can you imagine? She has her own e-mail address. She is so lucky.

Elizavoice and Bug are coming in after lunch for a short visit. It's a half-day at school and so they are coming in with my dad. I can't wait to see them. I feel so disconnected from everything at school and I hate that feeling. For now, I'm just going to take a short snooze.

. ⁓ .

"Look at this, Bug, they put her right across from all the action. Her room is right in front of the nurses' station. Isn't that wild! Maisey can see it all happen."

I can hear Elizavoice before I can even see her. Even the nurses are laughing. I'm sure my dad is ready to crawl in a closet. He creeps around here as if we were all asleep. It is pretty funny to watch.

Elizavoice and Bug check out every inch of my room. Elizavoice even tries to blow in my bubble thing, which she gets reprimanded for by the nurse because of germs. When the nurse is done, she salutes her saying, "On my honor I will be good in all hospital rooms."

It is so funny. Even the nurse laughs. I really enjoy the company, and they stay until about five o'clock, when Bug's dad picks them up. He is double-parked and the parking attendant downstairs is flipping out at him. Her dad works in Boston and has come over here on his way out of the office. What he was not prepared for was the traffic. He came in and out so fast that I hardly got a look at him.

When they leave, Mom and Dad wander outside the room again and begin having another one of those talks. I will be going home the day after tomorrow so I know that it is not about me. I can't believe I will be leaving without a brace. I am hoping that Tom will drop in one last time so I can show off my back. He made my bracing experience so wonderful. I think of him as an old friend, and I know I will miss him.

. — .

While I eat my dinner, Dad reads the paper, and Mom organizes my room a bit. Dr. Bones said that he would be coming by late because he had surgery today so I am looking forward to his visit. Just before he comes, Mom begins looking at her watch as if she is expecting someone. Then, without my even knowing they were coming, Charlotte and her parents appear. Before I can say much to Charlotte, Dr. Bones arrives. He asks Charlotte and her parents to excuse him and pulls the drape to check out my incisions. Charlotte asks if she can look. Although I am excited that she is interested, I am also surprised. In fact, it seems as if she has met Dr. Bones before. And no one introduced her parents to him either when he came in the room.

After Dr. Bones is finished, he looks over at Charlotte and says, "And how are you doing young lady? It's Charlotte, isn't it?"

Before Charlotte can answer, her parents come toward Dr. Bones as if they know him. Then something happens that I never thought I would see, much less hear.

Dr. Bones, I am sorry to take up your time when I know you are doing your rounds, but Charlotte's mom and I have finally made a decision. We have reconsidered the brace and have decided that we do want Charlotte to wear the back brace you suggested. We will be calling your office to set up a time to arrange for this."

I can't believe my ears. Charlotte never once said anything about her back. Now it is all finally fitting together: her questions about my brace, her interest in my surgery, and even her questions about whether I liked going to Dr. Bones and who Tom was. And most of all, those long talks my parents were having, especially the one with Charlotte's parents.

Dr. Bones looks over at them and says, "I was hoping that you would come around. It is never easy to make a medical decision about your child, and as a doctor, my hope is that it will be a decision made in the best interests of the child."

As Charlotte's parents and mine follow Dr. Bones to the door of my room, Charlotte leans over and whispers, "Maisey. I had scoliosis even before you did."

Dr. Bones looks over at us and says, "See you tomorrow, Maisey, and keep up the good work."

I know exactly what he means.

Epilogue

Maisey recovered very nicely from her spinal fusion and a year later was doing all the things she had done before her surgery. Charlotte was in a back brace within weeks after Maisey's surgery and wore the brace twenty-two hours a day for almost three years. Although her parents read an article about "nighttime-only" bracing, Dr. Bones explained that research indicated that the correction would not be possible this way. "Nighttime-only" bracing works poorly and research clearly shows a direct correlation between the number of hours a day a brace is worn and the likelihood of curve increase or eventual surgery. Charlotte was absolutely thrilled the day her X rays indicated that the bracing had successfully stopped the progression of her curve. No one was happier for her than Maisey.

It is important to remember that children who are not braced have about a two-in-three chance of having their curve progress, whereas those who are braced have only a one-in-three chance. Just as Dr. Bones shared with Maisey early on, bracing has been extremely successful in the treatment of idiopathic scoliosis.

If you yourself have scoliosis and are in a brace, it is important that you stick to the amount of time your doctor has asked you to wear the brace. You also need to keep up your appointment schedules with your orthopedist. If the brace is uncomfortable in any way, be sure to call your orthotist so that the proper adjustments can be made. Braces are comfortable when properly fitted. Charlotte is a wonderful example of the many successes of bracing.

Joe Demb Photography, Belmont, MA

About the Author

Mary Mahony is an elementary-school resource teacher and lives with her husband, Kevin, in a suburb of Boston. Mary is the mother of three grown children: Breen, an architect who lives in New York City; Colin, an analyst in Cambridge, Massachusetts; and Erin, a college senior. Mary enjoys revisiting some of the humorous things that have happened to her own children and weaving them into her writing. Her first book, *What Can I Give You*, chronicles her daughter's journey with congenital scoliosis. A strong advocate for children, Mary has spent many years working with families whose children are experiencing their own medical journeys.

Recommendations

"Mary Mahony has critically looked at the experience and problem of a teenage daughter with a congenital spine deformity. There are different forms of scoliosis and bracing is great for some, of borderline value for some, and totally useless for some. Congenital spine deformities are seldom responsive to brace treatment, whereas the more common idiopathic scoliosis does respond well in a majority of patients. Mary also impresses upon the reader the value of the second opinion (and even third) as well as the great benefit of well-planned and well-executed spine surgery. Mary has learned much of this from her own personal experience with her daughter, Erin."

Robert B. Winter, M.D.
Clinical Professor, Orthopedic Surgery
University of Minnesota

"Warm, sensitive, and real ... a book that any child can enjoy, and every patient, family, and caregiver dealing with scoliosis should read."

Joe O'Brien, Patient, and President,
National Scoliosis Foundation

"Mary draws upon her experience as the mother of a child with progressive scoliosis to offer keen insight into how a child feels as she journeys through scoliosis treatment. An engaging story for preadolescents, this book is also a wonderful resource for clinicians, educators, families and everyone touched by scoliosis, especially those of us with an 'S' on our back."

Thomas H. Colburn, Certified Orthotist; Director of Orthotics
and Prosthetics, NOPCO Boston; Chairman of the Spine Society,
American Academy of Orthotists and Prosthetics

"Watching Maisey confront the onset and progression of scoliosis while coming of age is a journey that evokes every emotion. Mary Mahony has depicted some wonderfully human characters and has captured preadolescence perfectly. This book will warm your heart and serve as an inspiration."

Nan Braucher, School Principal (retired)